NEWCASTLE UNITED GREATS

NEWCASTLE UNITED GREATS

JOHN GIBSON

SPORTSPRINT PUBLISHING
EDINBURGH

John Donald Publishers Ltd.,
138 St. Stephen Street, Edinburgh EH3 5AA.

ISBN 0 85976 765 3

Phototypeset by Beecee Typesetting Services
Printed in Great Britain by Bell & Bain Ltd., Glasgow

Acknowledgements
Many thanks to the Newcastle Chronicle and Journal Ltd
for the use of photographs in this book.

Contents

Introduction

Picking the ten greats of Newcastle United is akin to trying to scale Everest in a black and white pom-pom hat and a pair of sandshoes. It's well-nigh impossible because there have been so many fabulous players over almost 100 years. But it's also fun and in conjuring up my final ten I've tried to go for players within nearly everyone's living memory.

I've looked at those fortunate enough to wear the famed black and white shirt since the Second World War and selected players I've known personally and who have thrilled me as well as the many other thousands of United supporters. It's taken many hours of deep thought and elimination before coming up with my special heroes and if I've offended anyone by leaving out their personal favourite, then I'm truly sorry. I've left out a few of my own, too, simply because of the need to curtail a list which could have been almost endless. Newcastle United are indeed lucky to have had such a rich heritage. But then the North East of England has always been steeped in footballing tradition. It's reckoned that 10,000 folk would turn up to watch the washing dry at St. James's and I'm not so certain that isn't correct for, regardless of honours won, the crowds always flocked to 'the shrine' breathing the air of optimism. Certain of my selections are obvious. Could a Newcastle Hall of Fame ever be concocted without the legendary Wor Jackie or SuperMac, for example? They are merely nicknames but they're enough to bring instant recognition and admiration. Jackie Milburn and Malcolm Macdonald may have been two decades apart but they were so very much alike . . . both centre-forwards of blistering speed, both spectacular goalscorers, and both England internationals capped while with United.

It would be impossible, too, to consider United greats and leave out Kevin Keegan, who almost single-handedly in the early eighties turned the side from a run-of-the-mill Second Division one into a team which won promotion with panache and real flair. Keegan, a former captain of England, was a sensational and totally unexpected signing who justified every penny he earned by capturing the hearts of all Tyneside. He stayed for only two years but his impact was incalculable as he attracted other internationals to St. James's and led by shining example.

Two Geordie-born players who reached maturity under the guidance of Keegan and formed a lethal front partnership with him — Chris Waddle and Peter Beardsley — also deserve inclusion in my opinion. United, despite their obvious stature, had found it difficult to produce Englishmen capable of being capped by their country while still a Magpie. After Wor Jackie we had to wait until SuperMac and after him until first Waddle and then Beardsley (Keegan arrived as England skipper but never got a solitary cap at Newcastle).

Five down and five to go. That's when it became hard because the other candidates were plentiful, each with pedigrees to match the others.

If we had been going back to the mists of time there are those who shine like a beacon. In United's great Edwardian period at the beginning of the century United boasted an Irish full-back called Bill McCracken who was so adept at seeing off the opposition that the Football Association had to actually change the offside law to stop him strangling the game. There were others, romantics such as goalkeeper Jimmy Lawrence, who still holds the club record for the aggregate number of appearances with 495, the immaculate Colin Veitch and the long-striding Peter McWilliam.

As the twenties unfolded two legends named Stan Seymour and Hughie Gallacher emerged centre-stage, in the thirties came Jack Allen who gained immortality by scoring the 'over the line' goal in the 1932 Cup final against Arsenal, and in the early forties Albert Stubbins, whose goalscoring feats were sadly contained in the main to wartime football.

Before we move on, just a word or two more about those two little 'giants' Seymour and Gallacher. Each wrote his name into United's history in foot-high letters.

Seymour played in the 1924 Cup winning side and wee Hughie joined him when United lifted the First Division championship for the last time three years later. Stan, a left winger who won two unofficial England caps, later made his real mark as the man behind United's three Cup successes of the early fifties. He became regarded as Mr Newcastle, which was an apt description for a man who shrewdly bought little-known players who were to go on to become household names. Seymour served as honorary manager, chairman and director for many years.

Gallacher . . . ah, there's a name to conjure with. He was tragically flawed but a genius nevertheless. Stories abound of his goalscoring feats, and if he often viewed life through the bottom of an empty beer glass, then it only added colour and charisma to his legend. The fans loved the volatile little Scot with the touch of velvet and the explosive power of a volcano. He died under the wheels of the York to Edinburgh express at Deadman's Crossing in Gateshead which, in its own way, only immortalised a player who had so much but was his own worst enemy.

Enough of the distant past, however. We're mainly concerned with the forty years or so since Hitler was finally defeated and our final five of the greats. Frankly, they could all be found from the list of players who helped bring the Cup to Tyneside in those joyous days of 1951, 1952 and 1955. Jackie Milburn was the jewel in the crown but how United sparkled in those years. There was the blue-jawed skipper Joe Harvey, a natural leader of men; Man Mountain Frank Brennan at the very heart of the defence; twinkle-toed Bobby Mitchell on the left wing; the Chilean bull George Robledo who plundered goals at the shoulder of Wor Jackie; pint-sized Ernie Taylor in the engine room;

the flair and aggression of Jimmy Scoular; and little Len White, arguably the best uncapped player Newcastle have ever had.

How do you differentiate between men of such stature? The answer is with difficulty and time. And, even then, it comes down merely to a matter of opinion.

So, once again my apologies to those of a different persuasion. After a lot of thought I've gone for Mitch, who with Milburn and full-back Bobby Cowell played in all three finals, for Harvey because of his influence both as a captain and later a manager, and White who really came into his own after Wembley and who I know has a special place in the hearts of Newcastle fans.

Moving on from the fifties the next major milestone, apart from the Second Division championship side of 1965 built round the half-back line of Stan Anderson, John McGrath and Jim Iley, was the European Fairs Cup-winning team of 1969 under the managership of Harvey. Stars? Sure, there were. Skipper Bob Moncur, a rock on which opposing forwards floundered, Wyn Davies whose aerial power terrified the Continentals, and Pop Robson who scored goals with almost monotonous regularity.

In lots of ways the mighty Wyn was synonymous with the Fairs Cup days. Certainly his brave, almost suicidal way of leading the line had Europe's best defenders in a lather, but in domestic competitions he never scored enough goals and, considering we're honouring other centre-forwards such as Milburn, White and Macdonald, I've moved away and taken a defender as my choice from United's only European success.

Moncur, built in the image of his boss Harvey, has two outstanding qualifications. Despite being essentially a goal stopper he scored an unbelievable hat-trick over the two-legged Fairs Cup final against the crack Hungarians Ujpest Dosza and he was good enough not only to be capped by his country Scotland but to be their skipper as well.

Moncur bridged the gap between Europe in 1969 and

the 1974 Cup final at Wembley by which time SuperMac was established as the Geordie super hero. But there were other players who also pulled at my heartstrings. Terry McDermott, who went away to Liverpool to become a European Cup winner and England international before coming back, plus those pair of midfield creators Tony Green and Terry Hibbitt.

Oh, how I used to revel in watching Green. Boyish in looks with a lilting Scottish accent, he was the world's worst in training with arms flailing and head rolling, but put a football in front of him and he was like a gazelle. His speed of thought and reaction left lesser mortals for dead.

Hibbitt was a similar pocket schemer. Belsen-slim, his left foot possessed the accuracy of a surgeon's knife and how SuperMac cashed in.

McDermott's midfield style was different. So much of his best work was done off the ball with lung-bursting runs from the deep and a sweeping finish at the end of it. He possessed a ready Scouser's wit and the enviable ability to stay out all night and then run the legs off his team-mates in training the following morning.

Joe Harvey signed all three and revelled in their ability to entertain through undiluted skill. He loved Greeny, supplied Hibby with an endless stream of fags, and watched Terry Mac develop into an England international. Quite a trio and quite a manager.

I deliberated long and hard over Green, a marvellous manipulator so quick over the initial five yards and with so much vision. I loved him almost as much as anyone but injury cruelly deprived us of his unlimited talent. He played but 35 first-team games for Newcastle in the mid-seventies which sadly isn't enough to squeeze him into my top ten. But I'll always remember him with warmth.

No, the final place must go to someone else. David McCreery, a titch with a heart bigger than his frame, possesses more than 50 caps for Northern Ireland, as a testament to his commitment. He deserves consideration but I simply can't ignore the claims of Paul Gascoigne, a kid touched by genius. Gazza has more patter than a fortnight's rain but he also has more talent, more charisma, than you'll find almost anywhere else in the country. Often misunderstood, he can encourage the tabloid Press to take him to pieces but the lad from Dunston is an entertainer in a world sometimes lacking a splash of colour. He also cost two million pounds at a time when he was still wet behind the ears, which speaks volumes for his rare attributes. So Gazza it is.

CHAPTER ONE

Jackie Milburn

He became known as 'Wor Jackie', and that tells all. The affection the Geordies feel for their own heroes is epitomised in that name. It would have been unthinkable for John Edward Thompson Milburn, the miner's son from Ashington, to play for anyone else but Newcastle United.

His Football League career began and ended with United and so it should. He wore the black and white stripes with a burning pride at a time when the Geordies were a force in the land. A destructive war behind us, Milburn and United emerged into the sunlight of Wembley to claim the F.A. Cup three times in five years in the early fifties. And it was Jackie, hair brylcreemed, dress immaculate and manners impeccable, who strode centre-stage scoring goals which had hitherto belonged to the fictional world of Roy of the Rovers.

It was a time when football's image was clean and friendly, when supporters mixed freely with one another and the banter was precious, and Wor Jackie epitomised that world. Not for him the vulgar gesture of defiance or the mass hysteria at a goal. A mere handshake sufficed.

His sportsmanship contributed to his aura. He never fouled knowingly and he intervened soothingly in hasty clashes. He was simply nice.

Yet the beginning hardly prepared us for what was to come. Sure, Jackie came from a footballing background. His grandad played in goal for Northumberland in 1888, his dad Alec could have signed for Spurs and another brother Tanner had four sons who all became full-backs with League clubs — Jack, George and Jimmy at Leeds, and Stan at Chesterfield. Their sister, Cissie, was later to produce two sons named Bobby and Jackie Charlton!

But there was no scurry to sign the young Jackie. He had no particular pedigree as a schoolboy and League clubs looked elsewhere in their search for talent. Indeed Milburn had to ask United to sign him during the war years at the not too early age of 19. But once a mate had written into the club requesting a trial for the pair of them things changed rapidly.

Jackie, stardom still a thing of his dreams, turned up with his boots in a brown paper parcel and ate his lunch (a couple of pies) sitting on the steps outside St. James's Park. In those days public trial matches were commonplace before a new season opened. The Probables would play The Possibles, which meant in reality the first team taking on the rest.

Milburn was amongst the also rans against the day's big stars or those of them who were still around in 1943 when the War took so many to far-flung battlefields.

He'd scored a couple of goals in his first trial and in the second wore the famous black and white striped shirt against his personal hero Albert Stubbins, a ginger-haired, fleet-footed centre-forward who had scored a cascade of goals in wartime football.

At half-time Milburn had done nowt. Stubbins had scored twice and Jackie's lot were three goals down. One of the club's old warhorses, Joe Richardson, warned him: 'You must do something this half, son, or your chance will have gone.'

It was a warning Jackie took to heart. Fired up, he went out and played like a demon as though his very life depended on it. The goals flowed . . . one, two, three, four, five, SIX! Yes, the shy kid from the Northumberland coalfields scored no fewer than six times in 45 minutes as the first team were hit for nine to mark the beginning of a golden era of goals.

The *Sunday Sun,* reporting on the public trial, recorded: 'A tall youth, he showed a great capacity for quick attack and opportunism. With training he could have a bright future.'

Winston Churchill shakes hands with Jackie Milburn before the 1952 F.A. Cup final at Wembley. Looking on is skipper Joe Harvey with Bobby Mitchell to Wor Jackie's left.

It turned out to be the understatement of all time, of course, as Wor Jackie shot United to a series of Cup triumphs and won 13 England caps at a time when one was a precious commodity with so many great players around and there were no two-minute appearances as a substitute to bolster if devalue your total.

Forty-eight hours after that public display of goal power the young Jackie was back at St. James's with his dad to meet the guv'nor Stan Seymour, who spent the war years building United ready for greatness.

Milburn recalled the meeting with clarity: 'The moment we entered his office Stan slid his arm round my dad's shoulder and led him towards the desk saying: 'Come on Alec. Let's have a drink.'

'Out came the whisky bottle and before long dad was pie-eyed. I was sitting in a chair immediately behind Stan when I suddenly noticed that he had his hand behind his back. In it were two five pound notes — my signing on fee — and he fingered them like a magician fanning out a pack of cards.I'd never seen so much money in my life and I was mesmerised. I couldn't sign quickly enough.'

That was on the Monday and the following Saturday — August 28, 1943 — Milburn made his debut in the first team at Bradford City. Because United were leaving on the eight o'clock train from the Central Station the club put Jack and his dad in an hotel in the centre of town.

The Milburns had never stayed in such a posh place and father and son sat up until one o'clock in the morning talking and smoking. They were in bed little more than a couple of hours before, too excited to sleep, they got up, opened the window, and watched as the dawn broke over a sombre, grey Tyneside.

Jackie played inside-left but Bradford's inside-right, a man by the name of Joe Harvey, scored a couple of goals as United lost 2-1. A week later in the return Milburn marked his home debut with a sweet goal struck with his trusty left foot from 10 yards out at the Leazes end. This time Newcastle won 3-2.

Milburn learned his trade at the knee of Stubbins, a centre-forward in the true Geordie tradition who scored a staggering 244 goals in 199 wartime games yet still managed to possess the humility and decency that was to become the trademark of his pupil. Albert could motor a bit but the speed of Milburn was such that, when they put on spikes together in training, it was the youngster who came out on top.

His was a master signing, but then Seymour was producing a hatful of them. Bobby Cowell, Ernie Taylor, Charlie Crowe, Harvey himself, and Frank Brennan all joined the Magpies to set up promotion to the First Division and the Cup triumphs at Wembley. United went up in front of a record average attendance of 56,351. There were 15,000 applications for the 1,500 season tickets and it took the players up to three-quarters of an hour to fight their way up the bank through the massing hordes and into the players' entrance. Happy, happy days . . .

That 1947-48 season marked a milestone in the Milburn career for, after playing at inside-left and on the wing, he was converted into a centre-forward. It all came about because Charlie Wayman was transferred to Southampton for £10,000. The manager, George Martin, was sitting around having a natter with Stan Seymour, Joe Harvey, trainer Norman Smith and Jackie. The subject of Wayman's replacement came up and Martin declared: 'Jackie's the man.'

'Naw, keep him at inside-left or on the wing,' said Smith, shaking his head.

'Aye, he's not good enough in the air for a centre-forward,' agreed Seymour.

Milburn was nodding in agreement. He'd played only once at centre-forward at school (usually he was a left-back or outside-right) and he'd missed a sackful of sitters. The experience still haunted him.

'They're right,' said Milburn. 'I'm not cut out to lead the attack. I'm happy where I am.'

But Martin failed to wilt in the face of such mass opposition. 'You're wrong, all of you,' he declared. 'I'll tell you something. Not only will Jackie make a centre-forward but he'll get a cap into the bargain.'

The boss got his way and Milburn lined up at centre-forward against Bury at Gigg Lane. It was a match which was to re-shape Wor Jackie's career. Lady Luck smiled on the lad from Ashington who was to be touched with greatness. The Bury goalkeeper George Bradshaw was carried off with a broken leg after only five minutes and Harry Catterick, later to pilot Everton to the First Division championship as a manager, took over between the posts. Milburn, faced with 10 men, got off the mark with a fluke goal, the ball bobbling between his legs, and went on to complete his hat-trick.

By the end of the season Milburn was United's top scorer

with 20 goals, 11 more than his nearest rival Geordie Stobbart, and the first of his England caps came the following season against Ireland at Windsor Park in Belfast when he replaced the legendary Tommy Lawton.

'George Martin saw something a lot of us didn't, God bless his cotton socks,' said Jackie.

His England debut was something Milburn never forgot. 'The side was packed with big names — Frank Swift, Billy Wright, Neil Franklin, Henry Cockburn, Tom Finney and Stan Mortensen — and they all came across in the dressing-room to have a quiet word of encouragement. All, that is, except the greatest of them all, Stanley Matthews. He never looked my way and I felt uneasy but once we were out on the field just before the kick-off Stan shuffled across to me and said: 'I didn't say much in there because it's out here that matters. Just get across to the far post when I have the ball and you'll be okay. Sometimes it'll hang when I cross it so give it time.'

'I duly noted the advice and it worked a treat. The first time Matthews got away down the right I made for the back post, positioning myself some 10 yards out. Sure enough, the cross came high and deep. Two defenders jumped for the ball in front of me but I waited a split second before taking off. The cross hung and they were on their way down as I was on my way up which gave me that little bit extra height advantage and my header whipped into the net as sweet as you like. I scored on my England debut because I listened to Stanley Matthews and we went on to win 6-2.'

Ironically, Milburn was to thwart the great man just a couple of years later when Newcastle United embarked on their Wembley joy ride. The 1951 F.A. Cup final was supposed to be the occasion when Matthews at last picked up the Cup winner's medal to complete his fantastic collection.

Blackpool were everyone's fancy, United were merely the opposition for the day. But how wrong people can be. Wor Jackie had scored in every round on the way to the

Wor Jackie in his England shirt and international cap.

final and no one, but no one, was going to spoil his magical moment.

Milburn scored twice, two goals of such contrasting styles and breathtaking accuracy that Blackpool and Matthews were not only swept off the pitch but out of the headlines, too. It was Milburn who was the master, the supreme craftsman at the very pinnacle of his career.

His first was a goal for the connoisseur. Wor Jackie picked up the ball on the halfway line and ran like a gazelle directly for goal. A million thoughts must have passed through his mind, he must have seen a hundred shadows of chasing defenders and felt their breath on the back of his neck. Simply in that situation there's too much time to think but Jackie, ice cool and 100 per cent sure of himself, waited for Blackpool goalkeeper George Farm to commit himself and then tucked the ball home in the gap he had unwittingly opened up. Like all great marksmen he didn't even wait to see the ball hit the back of the net, he knew where it was destined as he turned away.

Milburn's second was the spectacular finish, the one for the punters. Outside-right Tommy Walker pushed the ball to little Ernie Taylor and as he did Jackie yelled: 'Backheel it.' Ernie duly obliged and Milburn struck it from fully 28 yards for the ball to fly like an arrow high into the back of the net.

Football in those days was more gentlemanly and after his first goal Jack remembered Stan Mortensen going across as he returned to the centre circle to say: 'Jackie, if we have to lose I'm glad it's to a goal like that.' For Milburn it was a poignant moment — Morty had been a player at Ashington when Jackie was a small ball boy.

The world watched in awe as Milburn displayed his supremacy and actor Robert Newton summed up the feelings of everyone when he said: 'My boy, I would give that arm off by there (striking his outstretched hand across his bicep) and that arm off by there to do what you did. Every actor who was ever born yearns to dominate the centre of the stage, just once, in his career with the whole world watching him and you did it twice in one day.'

United went on to win the Cup again in 1952 and 1955 but Wor Jackie maintained that the '51 side was the best of the lot. So here it is: Fairbrother; Cowell, Corbett; Harvey, Brennan, Crowe; Walker, Taylor, Milburn, Robledo (G), Mitchell.

Only three of that team played in all three finals . . . Jackie, of course, right-back Bobby Cowell and outside-left Bobby Mitchell. In 1952 Arsenal were beaten 1-0 through a George Robledo header late in the game and

Manchester City were crushed 3-1 three years later, both times when the opposition was reduced to 10 men through cruel injuries.

The '55 final was remarkable for events both on and off the field. Manager Dougald Livingstone, who had fashioned revolutionary training ideas on the Continent, actually dropped Milburn for Wembley despite the fact that he was a match winner and had battled back from a pulled muscle in the stomach, a bad injury for a footballer, to equalise in the dying seconds against Nottingham Forest and lay on two goals for Alan Monkhouse to win the second replay. He preferred Len White but, when he submitted his team to the directors, it was torn up and thrown in the nearest waste-paper basket. Go to Wembley without Wor Jackie? It was unthinkable.

White actually made the final team when Reg Davies dropped out with tonsillitis but the damage was done as far as Livingstone was concerned. If he was living on borrowed time in any case, Milburn inadvertently hammered the last nail in his coffin when he scored after only 45 seconds, the quickest goal ever in a Wembley Cup final.

Stan Seymour, who had led the bring back Milburn campaign, pulled him to one side as the team headed for the tunnel. 'Go out and show them Jackie,' he whispered. Hardly had the words died away than the ball lay snugly in the City net. United won a corner on the right and Len White went over to take it. City's captain Roy Paul was standing next to Milburn as White placed the ball when he suddenly yelled: 'Bloody hell, I should be marking Keeble' and darted off to find a player renowned for his prowess in the air. Jackie was all alone as the ball was curled by White towards him and he rose to head unerringly past Bert Trautmann and into the net.

That's right, head the ball . . . something John Edward Thompson Milburn wasn't supposed to do too well. If he was the complete footballer on the ground, upstairs it was quite another matter.

However, Jackie always insisted that his heading wasn't

quite the joke it was supposed to be. He claimed he suffered throughout his playing career from fibrositis which made him terrified of jumping with someone in case his neck 'stuck'. If it did he was unable to do anything except lie in bed. His lovely wife Laura even had to clean his teeth for him!

But if he jumped alone he was fine. Hence his Wembley header when Roy Paul deserted him. Jack, playing with an injury, had done all that was required of him within the first minute. City were shot and skipper Jimmy Scoular took over as chief tormentor, spraying crossfield balls to Mitch that pierced to the very heart. City may have equalised but the magical Mitchell restored United's lead and George Hannah completed the scoring from 12 yards.

It was the rainbow's end . . . . the journey of a lifetime over. Milburn was still to win an England cap and still to lead his beloved Magpies for another two years but the cycle of success was over.

Like any great theatrical star, the secret is to leave the audience gasping for more. Never but never outstay your welcome. Wor Jackie, of whom so much was expected by so many, knew in 1957 that at the age of 33 the time was nigh to say goodbye. Only just before he died his father Alec had told him: 'Get out while they remember you with affection, son. Don't spoil things.'

Gentleman Jack had wowed them in Ireland when he played over there as part of the deal that brought that fine little inside-forward George Eastham to Newcastle, and Linfield had written asking if he fancied going across to Belfast as their player-manager. A part-time club, they offered Jackie a club house, £25 a week and a £1,000 signing-on fee which was almost akin to a king's ransom when it's remembered that United's most popular player, three times a Cup winner and England's centre-forward, had only just received a rise to £17 a week at St. James's. Despite his loyalty United still asked, and got, a £20,000 transfer fee plus a forward called Jimmy Hill.

In three years at Linfield Wor Jackie, now theirs, had

Jackie Milburn (left) heads the quickest ever goal in an F.A. Cup final at Wembley when he scores within the first minute from a Len White corner against Manchester City in 1955.

every pair of Irish eyes smiling. The club won just about every domestic honour possible and Milburn, playing a lot deeper at inside-left than in his Newcastle heydays, still scored 150 goals. What's more, he climbed new mountains.

Competitive European soccer, denied to United in their halcyon days, was in its infancy but Milburn became a Continental star when, as Irish League champions, he led Linfield out in the European Cup of 1959. A crowd of 41,000 turned up at Windsor Park to see the Irish part-timers beat Gothenburg of Sweden 2-1 with Jackie notching both the goals. The Swedes had been warned of his prowess despite his advancing years, and in the return leg they unceremoniously kicked Jackie upaheight to swamp the little people 6-1.

Such was Milburn's new-found adulation that he was selected for the Irish League against the Football League at Blackpool. The Football League included 'foreigners' such as Denis Law, John White and Danny Blanchflower but the star of the show was Jackie, by now almost 36 years of age. His performance brought a flood of offers to return to the big time in England but having drawn his £600 provident money he was barred from ever playing in England again.

His love of United remained as fierce as ever and he regularly flew over the Irish Sea to watch the black and whites in action. It was during the days of Charlie Mitten as manager, and Newcastle were to be relegated from the First Division. Indeed Jackie was in the crowd at Tottenham when United lost his old playing mate Len White to a ferocious tackle from iron man Dave Mackay. Newcastle won 2-1 that day but, looking back, it was the match which doomed the club to the drop because, without White for the remainder of the season, they crumpled like a deck of cards.

After leaving Linfield and rejecting offers from the likes of Partick Thistle Milburn spent a season and a half as player-manager of Yiewsley Town in the south of England before an ill-fated trip into Football League management with Ipswich Town.

Alf Ramsey, who had won the First Division championship in East Anglia, had left to manage England and gain a knighthood for winning the World Cup. He left behind a Fourth Division team trying to play in the First. There was no youth side and not a scout on the books.

It was a job for a tough guy, someone with a will of iron who would turn the club upside down. In realistic terms Jackie was simply too nice a man to survive. He kept them up in his first season but in the second Ipswich were relegated and Milburn, facing intolerable pressure he had never known before, resigned.

It was a bad, bad period for the likeable Geordie and it took its toll. After yet another defeat Jackie would sit in a darkened room brooding for hours. The side of his face swelled to grotesque proportions through worry and for the first and last time in his life Jackie, virtually a tee-totaller, turned to booze for solace. The gin bottle on his own admission was never more than an arm's distance away.

It said a lot for his niceness and kindness that when he resigned the Ipswich players threatened to walk out if he were allowed to go, but when a national newspaper offered him the job of reporting for them back in his native North East he was off like a shot. Jackie was to stay as a constructive journalist until he took early retirement at the end of the 1987-88 season writing on his old club, Newcastle United, as well as Sunderland and Middlesbrough.

North East football could never forget one of its greatest ever stars, however, and there were moments of pure nostalgia for him. In May, 1967 for example, 10 years after last playing for United, he was awarded a testimonial match at St. James's and a huge crowd of 45,404 turned up to pay homage. Wor Jackie brought along all his old Cup mates as well as current internationals like Nobby Stiles and Bobby and Jackie Charlton and topped them off with the legendary Hungarian Ferenc Puskas for a match which left him weeping tears of gratitude.

Thirteen years later, on July 4, 1980, Milburn was installed as an honorary Freeman of the City along with a great supporter of Newcastle United, Cardinal Basil Hume, the Archbishop of Westminster. To Jack it was better than a knighthood. His own canny folk had honoured him in a way he'd never forget.

Jackie to me was a gentle character with unlimited dignity . . . one who began as my boyhood hero and ended up a personal friend. As a young whippersnapper I'd walked the three miles or so from my home in Benwell with my uncle Frank past the Big Lamp with the crowds beginning to thicken and buzz with pre-match excitement, down Stanhope Street and into the Leazes end of St. James's Park. It was a pilgrimage to Mecca and while every man jack in a black and white striped shirt was a hero, Wor Jackie was a superhero. The footballer of every young boy's dreams.

At that time I would never have dared imagine working with him as a colleague. It would have been unthinkable to call him anything but Mr Milburn. Heroes are untouchable, aren't they?

But Jackie was very much a man of the people and as I progressed through cub reporter at the *Evening Chronicle,* on to Fleet Street, and then back to cover Newcastle United for the *Chron* he became not only a helpful figure of some considerable importance along the way but even a firm friend. So much so that in 1981 we wrote a book together called *Jackie Milburn's Newcastle United Scrap-book* which directly led to Jack becoming the subject of a 'This Is Your Life' TV scoop and me being the key person behind the scenes in helping to pull it all together without the great man finding out, of course!

It all began when a 'This Is Your Life' researcher, Brian Klein, picked up a copy of our book at Thames Television shortly after publication date early in the September of '81. His job was to find out who was about to become hot news and decide if he or she might make a suitable telly subject for Eamonn Andrews and his famous red book. Milburn, thrust back into the public limelight with the publication of a new book and with a rich background involving some of the greatest names in sport, was a natural.

As co-writer of the book I received a phone call from Klein at the *Chronicle* offices one afternoon. Jackie Milburn was under consideration for a show and would I co-operate? Yes I would. The idea was kicked around a little bit on the phone and I was sworn to secrecy. No one was to know at this stage including Jackie's family. Contact made with Newcastle, the whole idea was laid before Eamonn Andrews for consideration. He was the big

Wor Jackie greets Bobby and Jackie Charlton on the set of *This Is Your Life* in 1981 with Eamonn Andrews holding the famous red book.

cheese with the final say but as a man with a sporting background Jackie Milburn appealed enormously. The show was on.

The tricky bit, of course, is breaking the news to the wife. This is when any 'This Is Your Life' programme can collapse. It's the most vulnerable part of the whole three months it takes to meticulously piece together one half-hour show. If the missus says 'No' or tells her husband through sheer excitement, then there's no programme.

I was chosen to approach Laura Milburn a couple of weeks after that first phone call from Klein. It was quite a responsibility with such a huge telly show resting on my ability to get the right response. So how to go about it . . . that was the 64,000-dollar question.

It wasn't that easy. Jackie worked from home as a regional journalist for a national newspaper, and so guaranteeing that he was out when I phoned Laura wasn't so simple. Aah, but there was one golden time when the home-loving Milburn would be missing — 2pm on a Saturday afternoon when United were playing at St. James's!

The call couldn't be made from the office on an open sports desk with too many prying ears around, so I slipped off into the Saturday afternoon shoppers to look for a phone box. Laura was flabbergasted. All the doubts which must flood every wife's mind came tumbling out. Would Jackie like it? Would it be embarrassing, perhaps too sugary? Who would be the guests? And would they spring some guy Jackie hadn't seen for donkey years and didn't even know?

A few reassurances that Laura would be consulted all along the line and the fears began to melt away. I'd managed it. Her acceptance, albeit slightly reluctant, was the green light Thames needed and two researchers were promptly dispatched to Tyneside for a personal meeting with Laura and myself. This is where the format of the show begins to take place. Over four days at the Gosforth Park Hotel Brian Klein and his assistant Cathy Parnall travelled countless miles to interview not only sisters, aunts, daughters, sons and old school friends but the famous as well. United's manager Arthur Cox, Joe Harvey, Albert Stubbins, Bobby Cowell and top athlete Brendan Foster were all contacted.

A major decision with Milburn's programme was where to record it. Virtually every show was put in the can in London where Thames Television had a theatre booked for most weeks. But on certain dates when the theatre was booked for other things Thames did an outside broadcast. Brian and Cathy returned to London with the problem to be thrashed out at a 'This Is Your Life' conference but with a strong recommendation that a show so dominated by a Geordie flavour should be set in its own homeland.

That was agreed in principle and the interviews went on unabated. Raich Carter was filmed in Hull; Bert Trautmann, the Manchester City goalkeeper against whom Wor Jackie scored the quickest Cup final goal in Wembley history, was tracked down in Pakistan and agreed to fly into Newcastle for the show; and Bobby and Jackie Charlton both gave up speaking engagements in the south to share the great night with 'uncle' Jack. Even Cardinal Hume, fellow Freeman of the City, was more than anxious to pay tribute — 'what a scoop,' enthused Klein in a phone call to me.

By November 19, less than a month before the programme was due to go before the cameras at Tyne Tees Television on December 8, we were discussing under what pretence I would get Jackie to the studios and how we would assemble an audience. It seemed obvious that a programme about Jackie's new book was as good a peg as any. Tyne Tees sports editor George Taylor, who would be conducting the spoof interview, collared me at Roker Park before a Wednesday night game and we worked out our plan. We decided to call the show 'A Chance To Score' — an obvious reference to Jackie — and the programme that was never to be took shape to such an extent that more than 100 tickets were printed and distributed to the Newcastle United Supporters Club and the Newcastle Supporters Association. Now that we had Jackie Milburn and an audience, neither knowing that they were in reality to attend a recording of 'This Is Your Life', the stage was set.

My final task was to keep Mr. M busy on the day of the recording while Laura, his family and friends, attended rehearsals at the television studios. 'Whatever you do don't let him out of your sight for a moment', Thames Television told me. 'We don't want him stumbling into any situation which would blow the show at the very last minute.'

I recruited the help of United boss Arthur Cox in keeping Jackie occupied. A lengthy interview was set up in Cox's office at St. James's Park in which Wor Jackie, Arthur and myself discussed the new book in detail. Cod questions and answers were set up for us to use on the show that night. After a couple of hours with Arthur we trudged off to an empty Milburn household.

'The wife's Christmas shopping with my two sisters,' Jackie explained apologetically as he attempted to heat up two beautiful home-made mince pies for our tea. The deception had worked like a charm. We were off to the studios in Jackie's car at 6.45pm still discussing what could be said on 'A Chance To Score.'

Jackie was ensconced in make-up while I hurried down to the front of the stage to give a thumbs-up. Warm up comedian Alan Fox finished his spot and George Taylor emerged to announce: 'Ladies and gentlemen, Jackie Milburn.'

As Jackie strode through the audience to shake hands with the man who for the next half-hour was supposed to talk to him about his new book the red curtains behind Taylor swished open to reveal a beaming Eamonn Andrews ready to pounce. Jackie's face was a treat — you'd have thought he'd missed a goal from two yards in the 89th minute of a Wembley Cup final.

'I was flabbergasted,' he told me at the reception afterwards. 'I honestly hadn't the foggiest idea what was going on. My first thought on seeing Eammon was 'What the hell's he doing here?' '

It was a night of lovely warmth and affection; a gathering of soccer's greats past and present as well as the Milburn clan.

A few days later a Christmas card arrived at my house. It was from Laura and Jack and inscribed: 'Words can't express our thanks for getting Jack to the studio. Ten out of ten and an Oscar!!! Thank you — you looked great on TV.' I treasure that card to this day.

No one is infallible, of course. Age can make even the great bow the knee. Jackie, who had gone home to Ashington to live amongst his very own, was showing undeniable signs of ill health as the end of season 1987-88 drew nigh. It was enough to cause Jack to leave his treasured soccer scene, retiring from the *News of the World.* The Press box was to miss his glow.

Through the summer there was always the feeling of uneasiness about Jack's condition. An intensely private man who gathered his family round him like a warm red blanket, it felt merely too intrusive to inquire too deeply.

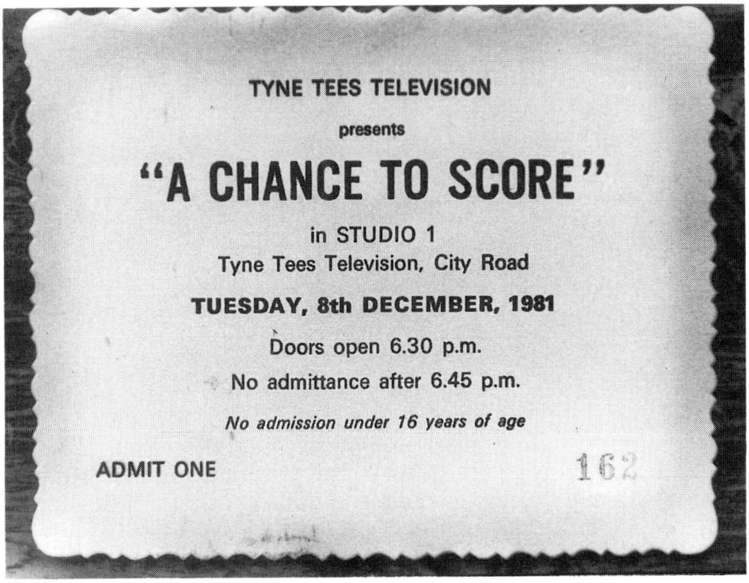

The show that never was — the ticket produced by Tyne Tees Television to get Wor Jackie and an audience to the studios so that the *This Is Your Life* surprise could be sprung.

But it soon became frighteningly apparent — Jackie had lung cancer.

He died on Sunday, October 9, 1988 aged only 64 years. We'd known what lay ahead — I'd had the unenviable task of writing his obituary in readiness for our tribute — but it was still like feeling a cold blade searing between the shoulder blades.

Tyneside was stunned. More than 30,000 lined the streets from his home in Bothal Terrace, Ashington to the cathedral in the centre of Newcastle. Heads bowed, eyes wet, the Geordies paid their homage and the national news on both TV channels showed the emotional pictures. Jackie's ashes were scattered over the Gallowgate end of St. James's Park where his most devoted fans used to congregate. The new stand, just finished, was officially named after him.

I was on holiday in Portugal when I learned of his death. A glimpse of an English newspaper read over the shoulder of a fellow tourist at the next table revealed the headline:

Huge crowds pay their final tribute to the great Jackie Milburn outside St. Nicholas' Cathedral in Newcastle at his funeral in 1988.

'A soccer legend dies.' I knew it could only be Wor Jackie. The rest of my short break was clouded and I flew home on the evening of Jackie's funeral — something which grieved me even more because I so wanted to be present to say goodbye to a friend.

Laura, as ever, thought of others even in her grief, and knowing how unhappy I'd have been at missing Jackie's funeral she asked me if I would like to give a tribute at a special memorial service which was to be held in Ashington itself. We all congregated in Laura's house . . . Laura proudly wearing one of Jackie's Cup medals, daughter Betty, son Jackie and the rest of the family, dear old Cissie Charlton, and Geordie Luke who used to play outside-left for Newcastle. Somehow it was a day of rejoicing in the happy memories rather than of sadness.

What I said from the pulpit probably lacked delivery and precision as nerves and emotion combined to play havoc with my stomach but it was from the heart.

'Aye,' said Cissie, squeezing my hand as I returned to my seat in the pew next to her. 'Wor Jack would have liked that.'

Nothing else really mattered.

'WOR JACKIE'S' RECORD

395 appearances for United and 199 goals (a club record).
13 England caps (1949-1956).
3 Football League appearances (1949-50) and an Irish League appearance.
F.A. Cup winner 1951, 1952 and 1955.
Second Division promotion side 1948.
Irish Cup winner 1960.
Irish Cup finalist 1958.
Ulster Footballer of the Year 1958.
United debut v Millwall August, 1946, scoring once.

CHAPTER TWO

Bobby Mitchell

Football once boasted wingers who were masters of the dribble, hugging the touchline to tease and torment full-backs and send over a stream of crosses for brylcreemed centre-forwards to bury with their heads. Stanley Matthews, Tom Finney, Gordon Smith, Jimmy Mullen, the more direct Billy Liddell . . . and Bobby Mitchell. The bobby dazzler had a left foot capable of opening a can of beans and a sway only matched by Marilyn Monroe. He was an artist who loved to create his own wondrous pictures but who, once removed from the football field, had little interest in the game.

Mitch was a doer not a watcher at a time when United were very much doers. He like Jackie Milburn lifted three FA Cup winner's medals in the glorious fifties to earn a privileged place in history. They don't make 'em like old twinkle toes now and more's the pity.

Bobby began quietly, inconspicuously, but trees from little acorns grow. He worked for Glasgow Corporation and almost everyone who knew anything about football on Clydeside never gave him a chance of making the big time. He was too skinny and too frail to succeed and had to try four Scottish junior clubs before he found someone willing to take him seriously.

'I hadn't played organised football at school,' recalls Mitch. 'We had a sports master who believed that soccer matches didn't foster the right sort of competitive spirit and my only games were the frequent kick-abouts with my pals on a patch of spare ground near our home in Glasgow and the occasional matches for the Life Boys movement which I joined.

The style of a master — Bobby Mitchell pulls the ball back before laying on one of his lethal crosses.

'I had left school when I joined the juvenile side of Market Star at the age of 14. I loved the game and my spirits soared when I heard that a keen supporter of Third Lanark had seen me and recommended me to the directors. Nothing happened, unfortunately, and I suffered the same disappointments when I tried to climb to the next soccer level — the junior teams.

'Market Star was the nursery side to Shawfield Juniors. But when I was given a trial I was advised: 'Stop where you are. You're too slight.' '

Mitchell was also rejected by Glencairn and Shettleston but, at 17, his first break came. Third Lanark gave him a run-out and asked him to sign as an amateur. Three days after signing he made his first-team debut against Greenock Morton.

'It was easier to make my mark because of the war,' he admits. 'It was 1942 and many players who would have been chosen before me were away fighting in the war. But it wasn't long before I followed them. Six months after my Third Lanark debut I found myself in a new role — as Ordinary Telegraphist Mitchell R., later to become Telegraphist Mitchell.'

He served in Malta, on HMS *Royal Scot,* a converted Scottish ferryboat which was used as the wireless ship to direct the South of France landing operations, and on an aircraft carrier in the Pacific Ocean. Back home at 21 he found himself at the crossroads in his career.

'Third Lanark wanted me to sign as a professional but I had my doubts. I wasn't fully convinced of my ability. For a while I worked as a clerk for an oil company. The call of football, though, was too strong and after a few months I turned part-time professional.'

In his first full season, 1946-47, Mitch was chosen to play for the Scottish League against the Football League at Hampden Park but against the likes of Ditchburn, Scott, Hardwick, Matthews, Westcott and Kippax the whole Scottish team had an off day and suffered a bad defeat.

The dandy winger with the dancing feet was creating a stir nonetheless, cracking in goals as well as making them and the big English clubs, hungry for rich pickings north of the Border, were beginning to take notice. Portsmouth manager Bob Jackson wanted him to sign and Bobby admits he would have done so had they allowed him to get a part-time job. Incredibly he still harboured doubts about his ability to make soccer a full-time existence.

Thank God he did because next in the queue were Newcastle United.

'I was training one evening at the ground when the

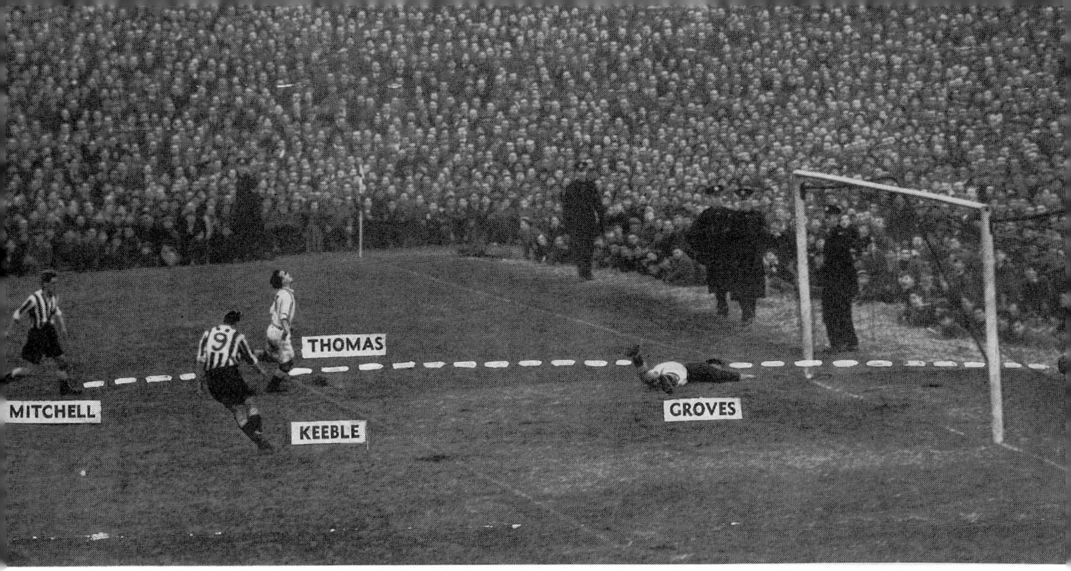

A typical Mitchell goal against Swansea at St. James's Park. Note the packed crowd.

Thirds manager Jimmy Carabine told me to hang around the boardroom. It transpired that Newcastle were negotiating my transfer. It came as something of a shock. I knew United were interested in me — the newspapers had been full of it — but as far as I understood Third Lanark were loath to part.

'But Thirds were never a rich club and they needed money. I learned later that the chairman, Sans Unkles, had convened a special directors' meeting to push my transfer through. He had chosen a time when all the directors against the proposal weren't there! Sans came out of the boardroom and told me the position. Then I met Stan Seymour, Doc Rutherford, and the Newcastle manager George Martin.

'I was well aware of the reputation of Newcastle United. They had just climbed from the Second Division to the top level. They had just had a big clearance selling Roy Bentley, Tommy Pearson, Charlie Wayman, Albert Stubbins and Len Shackleton and were rebuilding. Among the newcomers were the Robledo brothers.

'Would I go to Newcastle? Stan Seymour asked me. We discussed terms which were more than acceptable and then Stan lured me with some cunning bait. Newcastle were planning a tour of Canada and the United States at the end of the season and if I signed I would go. That settled it. I didn't know it then, of course, but I was signing a contract which was to bring me some of the greatest happiness it has been anyone's privilege to know in football.'

Within a few months that tour was to bring home to 23-year-old Mitchell the Newcastle lifestyle and the power of skipper Joe Harvey.

United boarded the ship at Southampton and discovered they had been put in the tourist class while Scotland's international squad were travelling first class. The senior players were annoyed and an emergency meeting was called.

'I sat on a bunk while the players gave their heated opinions about having to travel in such modest style,' says Mitch. 'Me? I was only too glad to be going. But the players insisted that they were Newcastle United and they deserved better treatment. Eventually it was decided to send a deputation to the directors with an ultimatum. 'Better accommodation or we don't play in Canada.' Joe Harvey saw Stan Seymour, who was the power behind manager George Martin's throne, and the next thing we knew we had orders to remove our gear to the posh upper decks.

'It proved how great the spirit of Newcastle United was in those days. The players were imbued with the traditions of Newcastle, they were told to be proud of the place they held, they were ordered never to give — or accept — anything which was second best.

'There were no quibbles from the directors. They were quite satisfied because they knew they could expect us to work ourselves to a standstill to uphold the name of Newcastle.'

Harvey's influence was paramount as United embarked on their glory years.

'When I arrived Harvey was like a father figure to me. He was the boss on the field and off it as far as the players were concerned. He sorted things out and did everything his way — nobody answered him back. Harvey was a great

The pants are long, the boots are high. But the grace and poise are timeless.

captain in the old style. He led his men magnificently. He had the qualities in him of the caricature Yorkshireman. He could be dour and dogged and didn't like being beaten.

'Some people show their sorrow more than others and I've never met anyone in the game who showed the disappointment of defeat more than Joe — and he had the ability to communicate this will to win to those around him. When things were going wrong he wasn't slow to make his point about just where he thought the weakness was. He talked straight and hard, not mincing his words, and the players accepted it. On the other hand, if there was any griping among the players he was the one who would take their case to the management. And he did it well.'

The year 1951 brought United their first — and probably greatest — F.A. Cup triumph against Blackpool and a fair slice of drama afterwards too. The celebrations were raucous, the champagne flowed, and chorus after chorus of 'Blaydon Races' echoed round the room. But too much champagne meant too much loose talk and goalkeeper Jack Fairbrother heard that a director had said: 'It's the last time he plays for us — he's finished now.'

In his heart Jack probably knew it was his last Cup final. He was over 30 and United had signed a bright young keeper from Third Lanark called Ronnie Simpson. But in his greatest moment it was a savage blow and Fairbrother's world crumpled around him. Harvey and Mitchell had seen what happened and when Jack went missing they scoured the hotel looking for him.

Then someone said they'd seen Fairbrother leaving carrying a suitcase. Joe and Bobby dashed across to King's Cross Station and found the keeper on the platform almost in tears. It took quite a while for them to persuade him to return to the celebrations.

'We had one match left at Wolverhampton in the League but we didn't care,' said Mitchell. 'We stayed at Lichfield the night before the game and continued our celebrations. Later Joe Harvey, Jack Fairbrother and I drifted off by ourselves. We decided to celebrate in every local hostelry. Jack set a cracking pace which we maintained throughout the evening.

'When we took the field at Molineux on the Monday night I'll swear not one of us was a true example of sobriety. Wolves attacked . . . and attacked . . . and attacked. But they couldn't score. Jack Fairbrother was positively brilliant. He picked them out of the air, off the ground, punched them, tipped them, did everything. And each time he got the ball he would turn to the trainer's bench where Jackie Milburn was sitting injured and bow!

'Wolves were wild. Then, to rub things in, we went up and scored minutes from the end to win the match.'

Defending the Cup is often the hardest part and it was magical Mitch who prevented them from going out at the first hurdle the following season — and then clinched a second successive Wembley appearance.

Mitch shakes hands with the Duke of Edinburgh before the 1955 Cup final. Next to him is Jackie Milburn.

United were drawn at home to Aston Villa in the third round and, like Humpty Dumpty, they looked set for a great fall. Nothing had gone right and with 10 minutes to go United were 2-1 down and the disillusioned fans were streaming home. Then Bobby Cowell got the ball on the halfway line and swung it across field to Mitchell. He was on the corner of the penalty area and — bang — the ball was in the back of the net like a flash. The Villa defenders were still arguing over whose fault it was when the same thing happened again straight from the kick-off. Across came the ball and Mitchell's flashing boot buried it deep in the net.

Right on time George Robledo completed one of the most amazing turn-rounds in Cup history and United had won 4-2. The BBC were inundated with telephone calls when their sports service announced the result late that afternoon — thousands of Newcastle fans who had left before the revival simply couldn't believe their ears.

Next were Spurs and they were beaten 3-0 with Mitch striking home an angled shot, and Swansea away, with Ivor Allchurch in their side, were also beaten by the Scottish wing wizard who scored the only goal of the game from 12 yards after outside-right Tommy Walker had supplied the ammunition.

If Mitchell had provided the early fire, 'Wor Jackie' did the business at Portsmouth in the sixth round. They were a marvellous team but found Milburn in irrepressible mood. Pompey went two up before Jack took over scoring what Mitchell described as 'the best goal I've ever seen.'

He gained the ball just inside the Portsmouth half in the middle of the field. He burst away and veered towards the left-hand corner flag. Milburn was challenged and on the angle of the penalty area when he unleashed his shot. No one expected it — the ball literally flew into the net with the keeper motionless. Jackie hit two more and George Robledo got another as United turned the tables 4-2.

The semi-final saw United draw with Blackburn Rovers at Sheffield and at half-time in the Leeds replay there was no score. Then in 57 minutes Brennan fed Milburn, the cross was met by the head of Robledo, and United were in front. However, Quigley put Blackburn level and the game see-sawed from one end to the other. The tension was unbearable. Four minutes from time Robledo launched himself at the ball and his header looked a winner all the way — until a Blackburn defender handled on the line. Penalty!

'The crowd roared and then hushed,' recalled Mitchell. 'Milburn was our penalty taker but he refused to take it — I think he had just hurt himself in a tackle. His deputy, George Robledo, also refused point blank.

'Joe Harvey came up to the penalty box and all the Newcastle players avoided his searching gaze. They didn't want anything to do with it. They started walking away. The crowd buzzed and Joe looked baffled. I don't think it occurred to him to take the penalty himself.

'By now I was feeling decidedly uncomfortable, and almost embarrassed. So I walked up to Joe and said: 'Give

Bobby Mitchell drinks out of the Cup after the defeat of Manchester City with fellow goalscorers George Hannah (left) and Jackie Milburn looking on.

me the ball.' Joe stood there dumbly and passed the ball. I hadn't taken a penalty before in English football. Now our possible Cup fate depended on it. I'm told that Newcastle's players turned their backs and that Stan Seymour, sitting on the trainer's bench, hid his head and asked trainer Norman Smith what was happening.

'I knew what I meant to do and I did it. I rammed the ball low past the keeper's right. That was it. Wembley again.'

The final was a bit of a disappointment though United beat Arsenal 1-0. However, Mitch's finest hour was three years away — the 1955 final against Manchester City even if by then a new manager, Duggie Livingstone, was bugging the senior players.

Livingstone questioned the slide-rule passing of Mitch, marking his boot with chalk, and told Wor Jackie he wasn't kicking the ball correctly. Mitch and Milburn — the two great stalwarts of United's success!

'From a personal point of view I thought Wembley in 1955 was my best,' says Bobby. 'My only disappointment was that I was instrumental in putting City's right-back Jimmy Meadows out of football for good. It happened early on. I took the ball to the by-line and Meadows came with me inside. I feinted to cut through and then scooped the ball back quickly with my left foot. Meadows was already moving to prevent me cutting inside and tried to change his plans in mid-air. As I leapt over his legs and centred I heard him yell. The ligaments of his knee had gone. He was finished.

'But I still don't think the injury to Meadows gave us the Cup. I believe that if City had had 11 fit men we would still have beaten them that day.'

United had gone ahead in the opening seconds through Jackie Milburn's header only for Bobby Johnstone to equalise with a long-range header.

'City's outside-right Spurdle had dropped back to mark me and our skipper Jimmy Scoular began exploiting him. From his right-half position he began hitting over some devastating passes to me. Spurdle was unable, naturally enough, to position himself correctly and left me with yards of open space.'

Mitch made it pay when Len White gave him the ball on the left wing. He turned on a sixpence to take the ball away from Spurdle and jink along the by-line. Trautmann was expecting a cross and left a gap at the near post. It was to prove fatal as Bobby rammed an eight-yard shot through the space and into the net. That goal was the breakthrough and towards the end George Hannah got a third.

There were no plans, no systems or tactics in United's

Bobby Mitchell the publican after his playing days were over.

great days. Stan Seymour used to say: 'You're not a Woolworth's team. You're supposed to be able to go out and play so go out and play your normal game.' But if 1955 showed some cracks, the writing was on the wall for both United and Mitchell when Charlie Mitten moved in as manager.

'I knew it was the beginning of the end and one day Mitten asked me to meet Sam Bartram, then manager of York City, to talk over terms. I wasn't interested in moving and said so. Nevertheless I met Bartram and told him the same. Mitten wanted me to go and when I refused there was a fairly heated exchange between us. There was obviously little point in staying so I went to Berwick Rangers for two seasons and then took over as player-manager of Gateshead.'

Mitchell, who loved the ball played to his feet to tease and torment defenders, had played 367 League games for United in 13 seasons, scoring 95 goals plus 41 F.A. Cup matches yielding another 18 goals. Yet he won only two Scottish caps, being unluckily kept out of the international side by the legendary Billy Liddell of Liverpool.

In was in June, 1961 that he signed for Berwick but he returned to St. James's in October for a testimonial which drew a crowd of 40,960 and receipts of £6,300.

I had watched in awe from the terraces as Mitch weaved his magical patterns but I was a young cub reporter covering non-league Gateshead when he arrived at Redheugh Park. In two short seasons I got to know Mitch well. He won the North Regional League but it was in his favourite competition, the F.A. Cup, that he enjoyed a last fleeting success.

We went to Darlington in the first round at the end of 1963 and were four up at half-time — a wonderful feeling for someone with a non-league club on a League ground — before winning 4-1. In the next round it was away again to Carlisle United, who were going well under Alan Ashman. Again Mitch, now thicker of waist and playing in spells, turned it on for a short while to set up two goals and another momentous victory was in sight. Gateshead were leading 3-1 in less than an hour but eventually lost 4-3 with Hugh McIlmoyle, a fine centre-forward, notching a hat-trick. I remember on the team coach back home Mitchell giving Gateshead's poor centre-half Jackie Herron a right old rollicking.

But really management wasn't for Bobby Mitchell. 'The only way I wanted to be associated with football was as a player and when that was over I was ready to stop. I wanted no part of the pressures that a manager has to endure from spectators, directors and various advisers all of whom know better than you.'

Once finished with the game, Mitch never returned. Not even to watch United play at St. James's. He wasn't bitter, merely uninterested. Golf became his passion though Tyneside remained his home. He became a publican.

BOBBY MITCHELL'S RECORD

Signed for Newcastle United from Third Lanark in February, 1949 for £16,000 — a record for a Scottish footballer, beating the £15,500 Derby County paid Morton for Billy Steel.
367 League games for 95 goals plus 41 F.A. Cup ties for 18 goals. A grand total of 408 first-team matches for United, scoring 113 goals.
F.A. Cup winner 1951, 1952, 1955.
Two full Scotland caps.
Best season 1954-55 when he was joint top goalscorer with Jackie Milburn, netting 19 goals in 40 League appearances.
Debut v Sunderland March 5, 1949.

CHAPTER THREE

Len White

Jackie Milburn called him the best uncapped centre-forward in England. United's fans revered him and still do. At 5ft 7in tall he was a barrel of dynamite with his furious weaving runs and thunderbolt shots. A leader in the best traditions of Newcastle No. 9's.

Len was born in the little mining town of Skellow near Joe Harvey's home town of Doncaster and left school at 15 to go down the mines as so many did in that part of Yorkshire. He earned around £5 a week in the same pit where his dad was a haulage hand.

At school he was an inside-left (no 4-3-3 or 4-2-4 in those days) and represented Doncaster Boys before making his introduction to the Football League at Rotherham United via the Upton Colliery side. White was 18 when he joined Rotherham where he played 10 games on the right wing, scoring four goals as they won promotion from the Third Division North in season 1950-51 — the same year United were hitting the Wembley trail with a vengeance.

In the next two seasons at Millmoor he played on the left or right wing in the Second Division without becoming a regular. Twelve appearances for one goal in 1951-52 were followed by 20 League games and nine goals the following season up to February, 1953. It wasn't spectacular but the White trademark was emerging and it was enough to alert the bigger clubs.

White recalls his move to United with clarity: 'They originally didn't want me — they were after our right-winger Jack Grainger. He'd played well in a cup-tie at Newcastle and afterwards they offered £30,000 but it was turned down. I was watched a couple of times and after we'd played at Fulham in midweek our manager Andy Smailes pulled me on the train back from London.

'He told me Arsenal, Wolves, Portsmouth, Aston Villa and United were in for me and said: 'Do you want to go to Newcastle or Newcastle?' Andy was a Geordie and there was no question where he wanted me to end up. We'd lost 2-1 at Fulham but I'd scored our goal and done all right.

'I knew all about Newcastle. They'd won the Cup in successive years and had a host of good players. I jumped at the chance of joining them but it wasn't just because of their Wembley successes. The club houses at Rotherham were awful — there were two rooms we couldn't even live in they were so damp. We could only use the kitchen, a small room at the front, and one bedroom, and I had a little daughter as well as my wife Joyce to think about. After that the Newcastle club houses looked like mansions!'

White's transfer was concluded in the York Railway Station Hotel the following day after directors Stan Seymour and Wilf Taylor had opened talks in London. The fee was almost £13,000, a record for Rotherham, beating the £10,000 they had received from Nottingham Forest for centre-forward Ardon.

White's big chance to impress in the game at Fulham had come with Shaw injured. Grainger was switched to centre-forward and Len played on the right wing, a position where he made his United debut against Liverpool at St. James's Park on the Saturday.

United were undergoing a period of transition after 1951 and 1952 and the reserves to visit Manchester City on the day of White's debut included Ted and George Robledo, Tommy Walker, Alf McMichael and George Hannah. Walker, a flying winger who didn't like the physical stuff, was axed to make way for White, who was partnered by Billy Foulkes with Jackie Milburn at centre-forward.

Within two years White was to be a Cup winner with United but he was in and out of the team like a yo-yo in the week of the 1955 final. Duggie Livingstone was the new manager with controversial new ideas. The League season hadn't gone too well but White had made 29 appearances, scoring 14 goals, and had scored another two in the Cup run to Wembley.

'On the Monday before we went to Brighton for Cup training Duggie said I would be playing at Wembley,' White told me. 'He was leaving out Jackie Milburn, who had been having a bit of a lean time. But it was still a shock decision because Jackie was a big-time player who on a stage like Wembley was capable of winning the match in one flash despite his age.

'When Duggie told the directors, they were mortified. Stan Seymour couldn't contemplate playing in a final without 'Wor Jackie' and Livingstone's team sheet was torn up. Stan announced on the Wednesday that Milburn would play and I wouldn't. I was to be 12th man, which in those days meant nothing because there were no subs and therefore no chance of getting on during the game. I'd been really excited about playing, with my wife and all my family coming down to see me, and it was a bitter disappointment.

'But on the Friday night our little inside-forward Reg Davies went down with tonsillitis and Seymour told me I was back in the team. Really, looking back, it did me a bit of a favour because I hadn't time to get nervous.

'But I felt sorry for Livingstone. He had the team at heart but within 45 seconds of the kick-off against Manchester City his job was as good as lost when Jackie Milburn scored.'

In fact White helped to drive the nail into Livingstone's coffin by taking the right-wing corner which Milburn headed in.

'A lot of folk said it was a good corner but really it was a bad 'un which was turned into a good kick,' said White, a modest man who perhaps never fully realised how good he was. 'I was looking for Vic Keeble at the back post because he was the only player in our forward line who could head the ball but it dropped well short. Luckily Jackie was there and he beat Bert Trautmann with a superb header!'

United went on to win 3-1 and White recalls with relish:

Len White, a master goalscorer at work.

'Bobby Mitchell was brilliant. He tormented City with Jimmy Scoular sweeping great crossfield passes to his feet.'

United's '55 side was significantly changed from the '51 and '52 sides with, among other switches, Bob Stokoe in at centre-half for Frank Brennan.

'Bob and I were neighbours in Fenham and I've never known anyone who hated to lose so much at absolutely anything. We used to go up to Westerhope to play golf — Bob was good but I couldn't hit the ball 10 yards. If it stayed on the fairway it was a good shot for me.

'This day Stokoe decided to give me a stroke a hole to make it more interesting but by a fluke I beat him. He went barmy, throwing his clubs around and swearing at me something rotten. We'd taken sandwiches with us and in the afternoon we were going out for another 18 holes. 'You won't get a bloody start this time,' he told me. 'You can play off scratch just like me.'

'Bob won just about every hole and the beam was back on his face by the time we reached the clubhouse.

'But he was a good footballer. He never used to give Brian Clough a kick, you know, and reckoned if he had played against Cloughie every week he'd have been in the England team.'

White the winger was to become United's latest king of the centre-forwards when Milburn left to take over as player-manager of Linfield in June, 1957. But before Wor Jackie departed, Len's development as a quality First Division player was going on unabated as another Cup victory over Manchester City proved.

It came in a third-round replay at Maine Road in the January of 1957 when City were the holders. Milburn was out of the side and a youngster called Alec Tait, a part-timer and schoolteacher from Bedlington, came in at centre-forward for his moment of glory with White again on the right wing. On a muddy pitch Newcastle were 3-0 down after half an hour — Stokoe scored an own goal trying to clear over the bar, Bobby Johnstone netted a header from a free-kick and Fagan scored from a glorious through ball from McAdams.

United's cause looked hopeless but City folk reckoned without the famous Newcastle Cup-fighting spirit. Immediately after the restart United were awarded a penalty when Bill Curry was sent sprawling and wing-half

White evades Wolverhampton Wanderers keeper Finlayson on his way to goal.

Tom Casey smashed the spot kick home. With 16 minutes remaining Tait scored the goal of a lifetime to put United in with a chance. Just after Irish right-back Dick Keith hobbled out of the match, Reg Davies slipped the ball to Tait deep inside his own half. Alec went off on a splendid run, beating five City men before hammering an unstoppable shot into the City goal from an acute angle.

In the 86th minute Curry headed an equaliser to make it 3-3 but in extra time City again took the lead. If the red-headed Tait had taken the bulk of the early applause, then it was time for the entrance of Len White now.

A humming drive from White destroyed Bert Trautmann and, in a fever-pitch match, it was an unbelievable 4-4. Could there be any more excitement left? There could. Two minutes after his first strike White was at it again, unerringly forcing the ball home to stun and silence a crowd of 46,990. The Cup holders were out 5-4 on their own ground with White scoring the critical final two goals to turn defeat into glorious victory.

The arrival of Charlie Mitten as manager in June of 1958 brought a period of colour, controversy and eventual failure, but for Len it represented the zenith of his career. He formed an inside trio with Ivor Allchurch and George Eastham which has rarely been equalled, never mind surpassed, in United's history and went on to represent the Football League.

Allchurch, the Golden Boy of Wales, was bought by Mitten within three months of his taking over the Gallowgate hot seat to range alongside Eastham, who had joined United as an 18-year-old from Irish League club Ards, and White who was now switched to No. 9.

'It was a pleasure and a privilege to play with two such fine footballers,' said White. 'George and I knew each other's game so well and Ivor provided a fair balance on the other side. It was fantastic for me. I could hardly fail. The balls put through by Eastham were slide-rule.'

Two old Cup heroes, now departed, would travel back to Tyneside to marvel at the Allchurch-White-Eastham partnership. Joe Harvey, then in management in the North West, called them the greatest and Jackie Milburn would hop on a plane from Belfast to see United play anywhere in the country.

Eastham was blond and frail but he was a master schemer with a flowing passing game and the vision of a hawk. Allchurch, leisurely in style, could sweep passes long or short with either foot and had the kick of a mule. Between them the crop-haired White was powerful and explosive, the perfect finisher.

By November White was called up by the Football League and seemed on the verge of the England cap everyone in the North East believed was his by right.

'I'd been given a few days off by the club and was back home at my mother's for a goodbye party — my niece and nephew were leaving for Singapore — when I received a call from the club on the Monday,' Len told me. 'Nat Lofthouse had been injured and I had been called into the Football League attack for the match with the Irish League at Anfield on the Wednesday. I hadn't dreamed of such a chance. It was a marvellous surprise.'

White responded in the way all great players do. He scored a stunning hat-trick in a seven-minute spell at the start of the second half. Twice in three minutes he struck in his first big representative game and then sprinted 20 yards to smash home a fierce drive for No. 3.

Tyneside clamoured for his England debut in the next game against Wales at Aston Villa later that month but, inexplicably, the call never ever came though White was picked for the Football League again to face the Scottish League in 1960.

The most popular reason given for Len being overlooked was his height. Wor Jackie reckoned if White had been two inches taller he would have played for England, but when I put the point to the little Yorkshireman he wouldn't accept it.

'A lot of people said that but I've always thought if you're good enough you're big enough. I've still got a clipping to this day where Charlie Mitten says if I had been as tall as him I would have been worth £80,000 which was a heck of a lot of money in those days. I never understood that.

'I liked playing against big centre-halves because it often meant that they were sluggish on the deck. And I remember when I scored four for United against Aston Villa three of them came with my head. Playing centre-forward is not about height, it's about having the knack of putting the ball in the back of the net.'

White admits that not playing for England was a disappointment but he says: 'That hat-trick for the Football League stands out in my career even more than my Cup winner's medal. It was the ultimate highlight.'

A typical example of White at his very best came in a game against Everton at St. James's in November 1959.

United had won only two games at home and were down to 18th position when Everton arrived on Tyneside. The game was to start a tremendous revival and Mitten's side eventually climbed to eighth position.

In the first six minutes United were two up through rasping shots from the edge of the penalty area from wingers George Luke and Gordon Hughes. Five minutes later White sped through to net as Everton appealed vainly for offside. Eastham scored No. 4 from the penalty spot before half-time.

White, aggressive and direct, taunted the Everton defence with Jones unable to hold him and he beat goalkeeper Albert Dunlop in 49 minutes to make it 5-0. Allchurch netted 10 minutes later but as United sat back the lively Thomas scored twice to give Everton a glimpse of respectability. That was enough to shake United out of their complacency, and with the Merseysiders' defence as watertight as a lace doily White completed a fine hat-trick and Allchurch cracked his second of the day. Even then White hit the post before Everton were allowed to escape to the sanctity of the dressing-room smarting from a huge 8-2 defeat.

Len recalls Mitten with a smile. 'He was a real character brim full of new ideas. He took us to Barcelona in the close season and when we came back he changed all the doors on the lockers and swapped the square baths for round ones. He changed our strip, putting a white trim round the shorts, and experimented with playing styles. But he was essentially a players' manager.'

Scoular was still United's powerhouse right-half with the tackle of a beartrap and inch-perfect distribution. He was a hard man on the field and he let the others know it.

'In one game at Luton Scoular played a great ball over the full-back to Gordon Hughes, on the right wing just over the halfway line. Hughes was normally a flyer but he never moved an inch. Scoular bellowed: 'You bloody sod. Move yourself!'

'Gordon stuttered when he got excited and he was

Goalscorers supreme — Len White and Jackie Milburn in later life.

petrified. 'S-s-s-s-sorry, J-J-J-Jimmy,' he protested. 'I've got cr-cr-cr-cramp in both legs!'

'Actually, I think Gordon could have played for England if he'd had a brain. He wasn't clever but he could give even the quickest full-back 10 yards. The trouble was that instead of cutting inside going from the near post he'd run towards the corner flag trying to centre at speed and a lot of his crosses fell behind.'

White was a goal machine and he finished as United's top scorer in five successive seasons with the following totals: 1956-57 13 goals; 1957-58 25 goals; 1958-59 25 goals; 1959-60 29 goals; and 1960-61 29 goals.

It was in that last season that Len was going like a bomb until a cruel injury took him out of the firing line and led directly to United's relegation from the First Division and subsequently the sacking of Mitten.

'We went to Spurs who hadn't lost at home for quite a

few weeks and had a real go at them,' said White. 'In fact we were leading 2-1 when they got a corner. They were going to take it short and I noticed that Dave Mackay was moving up so I went with him. When the ball came over I managed to slip in front of him and the next thing I knew I crumpled in a heap. It was a bad foul and I didn't play again that season when we went down.

'The point is that, at the time, I was scoring on piece. If they didn't go in off my right foot they went in off my left. Newcastle's record League haul was 36 goals by Hughie Gallacher when they won the First Division championship in 1926-27, and despite us being in relegation trouble I felt I had a chance to beat that.

'I had 28 League goals in 33 games and with about a couple of months of the season still to go I was in with a shout.'

Jackie Milburn, who had travelled to White Hart Lane to see the match, told me years later that Mackay's tackle was one of the worst he had ever seen. Certainly in that moment as a limp White was carted off the field United's lights were dramatically switched off.

Len is far too polite to point it out, but while he was reaping goals galore his defenders were chucking them in at the other end. United scored an impressive 86 goals but let in a staggering 109 and were relegated along with Preston North End.

By October, with United lying 18th in Division Two, Mitten was sacked and a few months later — in February, 1962 — White's glorious reign at St. James's was over. The little man with the big heart had scored 153 goals in a black and white shirt in 269 League and Cup matches. He was to leave the area for good but his name has lived on and when I interviewed him for this book he honestly told me 'I could have remained on Tyneside for ever. I may be a Yorkshireman but for me Geordieland is a wonderful place full of warm, generous people.'

White left United for Huddersfield Town and a nomadic finale to his playing career. He also signed for Stockport

County and Altrincham, played fleetingly for Sligo Rovers in Southern Ireland and then, back home in Yorkshire's heartland, continued to play the game he loved at local level, defying the passing of time. Last season — 1988-89 — he turned out 'whenever the lads gave me a call' at the grand old age of 59 as a back four player.

'Stockport was a lovely little club,' he told me. 'I was just a player with them but I could do anything I wanted. I scored all three goals in my second game when we beat Wrexham 3-0, and from then on I couldn't do a thing wrong. I was made skipper and whenever the manager was away I took the training.'

There was a final moment of magic for White when Stockport took on the great Liverpool at Anfield in the Cup. They boasted the likes of Scotland's goalkeeper Tommy Lawrence, towering centre-half Ron Yeats, mid-fielder Gordon Milne and quicksilver centre-forward Ian St John, but little Stockport unbelievably held them 1-1 with, you've guessed it, White getting their goal.

'There were 51,000 in Anfield and we shocked them by taking the lead,' recalls Len, who was 38 years of age at the time. 'I remember the goal well because of the pain it caused me. The ball came off Lawrence's chest and hands and I nipped in to head it home. He was trying to punch it away and caught me a real whack, fracturing my ribs. I shouldn't have played in the replay but I desperately wanted to and I went out strapped up like a mummy.

'Milne didn't equalise until 15 minutes from time and it was a messy goal but they beat us fair and square 2-0 at our place in the second game.'

A fib took Len over to Southern Ireland for six months. 'Their manager phoned me and asked how old I was. I said 37 when really I was 40 but I felt like a kid.'

So how has he kept playing despite approaching 60 years of age? 'Because I enjoy it and still have the basic pace. I play a lot of tennis, and coming in quickly to the net behind my service keeps me fit. I'm as quick as anyone over 10 yards though I would probably be murdered over

100 yards by the young lads. My head and my experience coupled with my initial speed is enough to get me by playing at the back.'

White, like so many great stars, much preferred playing to anything else. He told me he only applied for one manager's job and gave up his only coaching appointment because he couldn't stand the agony of telling kids full of anticipation and hope that they weren't going to make it.

'Ray Wilson, England's World Cup full-back, took me to Bradford City to coach the young 'uns but after two or three weeks I couldn't take it. I had 14 and 15-year-olds three or four times a week but part of my job was to assess them and get rid of them if they hadn't what it takes. Many was the time I saw a young lad leave the ground with tears streaming down his cheeks. I wasn't right for the job — I could remember how much football meant to me as a kid and spoiling dreams wasn't for me.'

White rarely watches the game he adorned so brightly for a decade with United. 'I never go to League games though I'll watch a match on the telly,' he said. 'It's so different now — and when a team like Wimbledon can win something as big as the F.A. Cup, it tells you everything about what's wrong with the game today.'

Len White, ever the purist, prefers his cherished memories from a golden past.

LEN WHITE'S RECORD

244 Football League appearances for United, scoring 142 goals and 269 games all in for 153 goals.
F.A. Cup winner 1955.
Two Football League appearances, scoring a hat-trick against the Irish League.
Debut v Liverpool February 21, 1953.

CHAPTER FOUR

Joe Harvey

Joe Harvey had a jawline like a girder and a clear and uncompromising eye of the kind which can quell rebellion at 30 paces. He led from the front — captain supreme and manager of distinction. His life was all about Newcastle United.

With the enemy quivering on the point of surrender he was the commander who would step from his tent and demand the *coup de grâce.* No last-minute reprieve, no feeling of guilt or compassion at the height of the battle because that could produce losers not winners. He bullied United to Wembley in 1951 and 1952, led with a style that demanded his troops to follow him over the top. The great stars, the better players, never contradicted Harvey. His word was law on the park. Harv would growl like a sergeant major with toothache and no one raised an eyebrow in dissent.

United's skipper became their manager and later held a succession of lesser managerial roles as his love affair with St. James's Park refused to let him go. He mellowed, of course he mellowed, but he remained essentially a man of iron and pride.

He tasted the unrestrained joys of success both as player and manager. An adopted Geordie who relinquished his Yorkshire background for a life in which everything was black and white.

Joe made the journey which was to reshape his life early in March of 1945. It was from Bradford, where he played for the City team, north to Tyneside and a gathering of tomorrow's stars. Four thousand two hundred and fifty pounds changed hands as United got a leader of men.

In those days uncomplicated by soccer tacticians Harvey was a wing-half wearing the No. 4 shirt. In a team that was a subtle balance of power and finesse he provided the defensive strength at the shoulder of a granite centre-half Frank Brennan. Running into Joe was like hitting a bag of iron, and trying a different route via Brennan brought no more joy. Frank, a two and a half pound baby at birth, developed into a 6ft 2in, 14st giant of a man who would roll up his sleeves and tell his full-backs: 'Piss off, and let me get on with my job.'

Big Frank would eat 12 eggs and half a dozen rashers of bacon for breakfast with lashings of toast on top — and then eat the opposing centre-forward for tea!

It was Harvey's leadership which made him stand out from other men at a time when United were a force in the land. Players like Bobby Mitchell, Tommy Walker and Jackie Milburn used to get a bit lax on occasions and needed a touch of the verbals. Others such as Charlie Crowe, Bobby Cowell and Ernie Taylor sometimes needed a boost and Joe psyched them up.

Like a lot of hard men, Joe loved a player who could play. He admired skill, the deft touch, the purveyor of a defence-splitting pass, and consequently he loved little Ernie Taylor. He would stop in mid-stride when Taylor hit a raking pass and, hands on hips, exclaim, 'Ernie, there's not another man in the bloody game who could pass a ball like that.' You could see Taylor's chest puffing out with pride.

Joe always believed that Taylor, knee-high to a grass-hopper, was an England player, and when he finally got an international call against the great Hungarians Harvey travelled to London to stand on the Wembley terraces and support his little mate.

Ronnie Simpson, the goalkeeper with the spidery legs and the agility of a gymnast, recalls the Army style of Harvey when, during the 1952 Cup final against Arsenal which saw United win a tight game by the only goal, a free-kick was conceded on the edge of the Newcastle penalty area. As the wall lined up Harvey bellowed: 'Simpson, let this one in and you'll be thrown in the bloody Tyne.'

Joe Harvey in typical battling style.

Simpson admitted years later: 'I was honestly scared because if Arsenal had scored I'd have had to face Joe. There was no way I was going to be beaten under those circumstances.'

By the time United returned to the twin towers three years later Harvey had retired and been appointed first-team coach. His name may not have gone on the roll of honour but his influence was still supreme. A lot of the old names had gone and new manager, Dougald Livingstone, had brought not only fresh ideas but a disruptive influence into the camp. There was a huge gulf between the senior players and the manager and 'Wor Jackie' recalled: 'It was

Joe who bridged that gap. We all thought the world of him and he used to say "Forget anything else. It's up to you lot on the field. You decide what really happens".'

What happened is that United lifted the Cup yet again with Milburn and Mitchell, never Livingstone men, playing a significant role.

Harvey was managerial material without a doubt but he had to leave St. James's Park to cut his teeth. He heeded the call 'go west young man' and learned his trade at Barrow and Workington in the lower divisions before returning 'home' in the summer of 1962 never to leave again. The pull of Geordieland was so great for the Doncaster-born Harvey that he was on the point of quitting soccer altogether to bring Ida and the kids to Newcastle when his old club conveniently opened the door to him.

His contract at Workington was about to run out and a restless Joe had informed the board that he would be leaving. His haven was to be a little sweet shop on the West Road in Newcastle. Indeed Ida was already back in the city and Joe was living in digs while he saw out his contract when the call came. Had it not, United might never have sampled the success ahead and Harvey might have been selling sweets to kids for the rest of his natural life.

A lot had happened to United since Harvey departed — and not much of it was good. Charlie Mitten, a gambler by nature, had tried a big throw of the dice and come up with a big fat zero. He'd taken Newcastle into the Second Division on the back of a record which saw 86 goals scored but an incredible 109 conceded. Six months later he was sacked. Norman Smith, the old Cup final trainer, spent a few months in charge as a stop gap team manager before Harvey was summoned.

What confronted him was a mess. Too many players were uninterested in what was going on. Everything was lax. The place carried the stench of mediocrity, yet in the next 13 years Harvey was to win the Second Division championship, the European Fairs Cup, reach the F.A. Cup final, produce a couple of Texaco Cup wins and lift the Anglo-Italian Cup as well as pilot the Magpies through

A proud Joe Harvey holds the Cup aloft after United had beaten Arsenal 1-0 in the 1952 final at Wembley.

three lucrative years in Europe. In the process Harvey built three different teams, assembling the Second Division championship side around a half-back line of Anderson, McGrath and Iley, the Fairs Cup team around Davies, Robson and the defensive qualities of Moncur, and the Wembley side around SuperMac.

He took what he'd shown on the pitch into the manager's office and added that special ingredient so vital to a boss: the ability to spot and sign real talent.

Harvey displayed that trait right at the very start of his managerial career with Newcastle. He knew he needed an inspirational skipper, someone who could get hold of the side in midfield and pull it together. That man was Jim Iley, bought from Nottingham Forest for £16,000. He later brought Stan Anderson from Sunderland for £3,000 more and revitalised the career of John McGrath, and United went back up to the top flight as champions in 1965.

But then Harvey could always buy. He went on to sign such gems as Terry Hibbitt from Leeds reserves, Terry McDermott from the obscurity of Bury, Malcolm Macdonald who had never kicked a ball in the First Division, and the irrepressible Tony Green. The man who had admired the skills of Ernie Taylor never lost his feeling for the artists of football.

Joe the manager was someone I got to know well. Just a year after United were Second Division champions I returned from Fleet Street to cover Newcastle for the *Evening Chronicle* and remained with him until he eventually stepped down. They were happy years travelling the length and breadth of Europe and Harvey was an inspirational force at the helm. His transfer market manipulation was coupled with shrewd man management and the ability to appoint good coaches — Jimmy Greenhalgh in the promotion year, Dave Smith in the Fairs Cup and Keith Burkinshaw for Wembley.

We were a happy if somewhat naive bunch in the old Fairs Cup days. Victory was commonplace, defeat something which never honestly crossed the mind. Joe's battle-cry whenever something small used to go wrong was 'It'll be all right on the night.' Invariably it was.

The draw was always eagerly awaited and when it came Harvey, accompanied by a posse of Press men, would be off to watch the opposition. These spying trips became a joy, something which brightened up the winter months of battling through the snow to the likes of Southampton and Crystal Palace. Joe was the perfect host. Many's the time I've seen him go behind the bar in Lisbon or Brussels to pull us all a pint after closing time. Many's the meal I've enjoyed in a Continental restaurant where we'd select our own lobster swimming in a tank before it was served up to us piping hot.

The spying itself was little more than a promotional exercise. I remember going with Joe to Como, a little town

Joe Harvey the manager lifts the European Fairs Cup to the skies after United's triumph over Hungarians Ujpest Dosza in 1969.

on a beautiful lake in northern Italy to watch the great Inter Milan in action.

Programmes are a rarity in Continental football and I made my way to the dressing-rooms to get the Inter team before taking my seat next to Harvey in the stand. Throughout the match Joe, smoking fag after fag, cracked jokes never once making a note or asking a player's name. Afterwards he came out with enough emotive quotes to satisfy my sports editor back in Newcastle and, mission over, it was back to Tyneside for business as usual.

A couple of weeks later we flew out to Milan for the tie and, on the morning of the match while I was still filing my copy to the office, there was a loud banging on my bedroom door. It was Joe.

'Bloody hell, Gibbo, have you still got a copy of Inter Milan's team from Como?' he asked me in a sweat. 'We've got a team meeting and I've got to tell the lads something!'

It sounds daft, even comical, but Harvey was no fool. His philosophy was simple: make certain United got it right and let the opposition worry about you. He didn't fill the players' heads with fear or detailed plans to halt the opposition. He kept it simple, played to United's strengths, and dismissed the foe in a few short sentences. He'd seen them play, they were a decent side, but we were better. And the players believed him — after all, he'd been out spying, hadn't he?

I always remember much later Malcolm Macdonald, brought up on the Harvey doctrine, thinking Don Revie was crackers for handing England players dossiers as thick as a navvy's sandwich on the opposition. 'By the time you finished reading them you thought you were playing 11 supermen,' said Macdonald. 'It was ridiculous. In the end I used to throw mine away.'

United, as usual, produced a result in the magnificent San Siro Stadium, drawing 1-1 with Inter Milan and then dispatching them 2-0 at St. James's.

Even in Newcastle's biggest-ever European game, against Hungarian masters Ujpest Dozsa, in the Fairs Cup final, Harvey remained the complete optimist at the one time when the tide of battle seemed to be running against him. Before a capacity crowd at home United had carved out a convincing 3-0 scoreline with two Bob Moncur goals and another from Jim Scott but, after 45 minutes in Budapest, that lead was savagely eroded.

They had scored twice with United hardly getting over the halfway line. I was sitting next to Len Shackleton, the old Newcastle and Sunderland star, in the Press box and we feared the worst. 'Uj-pest, Uj-pest' the chants rolled round the stadium as the crestfallen United players trudged off to the temporary sanctum of the dressing-room.

Once inside they sank in their seats. David Craig, a marvellous right-back whose career was blighted by injuries, sat next to Bob Moncur, their heads down. Sweat dripped off their foreheads. No one spoke.

Then the door burst open. It was Harvey. Looking round the room, as silent as the grave, he started . . .

'Listen you lot, you're bloody winning. Winning I tell you. You're bloody 3-2 up in a cup final with only 45 minutes to go. What's up with you. Hit 'em once early on and they'll collapse. These Continentals are all the same. One goal and we've got the pot.'

Tactics weren't necessary at this stage. What was wanted was a Churchillian speech to lift flagging souls. It was ready made for Harvey.

Moncur recalls looking at Craig. Had the gaffer gone mad or was he, perhaps, right? Maybe, just maybe, there was a chance.

Out went United with Harvey shaking his fist under each and every player's nose. One last effort . . .

United went forward from the kick-off. They won a left-wing corner, goalkeeper Szentmihalyi punched clear little Jackie Sinclair's flag kick, and when the Scot returned the ball there was Moncur to thunder a shot home. 4-2 on aggregate!

Up in the Press box I could see the confidence drain from every Magyar face and the self-belief pouring back into the Geordies. Harvey was right. Spot on. Ujpest folded, United became stronger, and they ran out 3-2 winners on the night to take the cup easily on a 6-2 aggregate.

Afterwards we sang and drank in the dressing-room. All of us, the Press, the players and the Newcastle officials. In the middle of the mayhem I caught sight of Joe sitting in the corner, his face wreathed in smiles. He winked and I nodded back, well chuffed. Harvey had done his job, the one he was best at.

Our relationship was a good one. As the local reporter Joe knew I had a job to do and respected that. He was also willing to take me into his confidence knowing that we both wanted the same thing — a successful Newcastle United. Often he would point me in the right direction on team changes. He'd tip me the wink and I'd carry the story without quoting him. It was give and take — I'd not print a story on a possible transfer target until the right moment in case it affected his chances of getting his man. That was the perfect manager-Press relationship, something subsequent managers didn't realise or weren't prepared to exploit.

But the team tip-offs led to one bit of trouble. The players felt they learned what was going to happen by reading the *Evening Chronicle* — I was right far too often for it to be an educated guess — and everything blew up on a trip to Southampton.

The team went early, and when I followed on an anxious Harvey was waiting for me by the hotel entrance.

As I walked in he grabbed me by the shoulder and dragged me into a nearby room.

'Gibbo,' he said. 'You know nowt. There's been a team meeting and the lads have accused me of telling you the team before they know. Play dumb.'

A nod's as good as a wink to a blind horse and when the players approached me I strongly denied knowing any inside gen. It was a matter of putting two and two together and coming up with four. A crisis was averted.

But, as I've said, it was give and take with Joe. And I did him a big favour just before the 1974 F.A. Cup final. When he announced the team a couple of days before Wembley, he'd decided to play Jinky Smith out wide on the right and leave out his natural winger Stewart Barrowclough. Barra, naturally, was devastated and his first reaction was to pack his bags and go home. I got wind of it and went straight up to Stewart's bedroom. It was a belting story — Cup final star walks out on team — but Stewie was a good mate and Harvey needed trouble right then like a hole in the head. The story wasn't worth it and I spent a good hour persuading Barrowclough that all he'd get from such a

United may have lost the 1974 F.A. Cup final to Liverpool but Harvey is still lifted shoulder high by fans on the team's return to St. James's Park.

walk-out was trouble. Eventually he saw sense and decided to stay. The story never got out.

By the end of the following season — 1974-75 — Harvey had resigned and an era had come to an end. Apart from a short break he stayed on holding various posts such as scout, chief scout and assistant manager, unable to give up totally the club which was now imprinted on his heart.

The new manager was Gordon Lee, brought from the Third Division where he'd worked with Blackburn Rovers. It was a culture shock after Joe. Whereas Harvey loved characters, Lee hated the star system. Joe had treated Malcolm Macdonald like a son, Lee felt he was a bighead and clashed with him immediately.

Lee sold Terry Hibbitt, SuperMac's provider, to Birmingham City within half an hour of the final whistle after a match at Derby County and got rid of SuperMac himself to Arsenal. That was bad enough but when Lee eventually quit himself to go to Everton with the job unfinished the fans went wild.

If Harvey had been one of the most popular managers ever, then Lee was destined to be known as one of the most hated.

Joe, still employed by United, died of a heart attack on Friday, February 24, 1989. He was 70 years of age. Appropriately the end came with him sitting chatting to his old '50s Cup final mate Bobby Cowell. He went out as he had lived life — with a smile on his face talking about football.

JOE HARVEY'S RECORD

245 appearances for United and 12 goals.
Three Football League appearances 1948-52.
Second Division promotion side 1948.
F.A. Cup winner as captain 1951, 1952.
United debut v Millwall away August 31, 1946.

AS MANAGER

Second Division champions 1965.
European Fairs Cup winner 1969.
F.A. Cup finalists 1974.
Anglo-Italian and Texaco Cup winner.

CHAPTER FIVE

Bob Moncur

The similarities between Bob Moncur and his manager Joe Harvey were there for all to see. Both were no-nonsense defenders hewn out of granite, both swarthily dark-haired and good-looking, both leaders of men who knew what it was like to lift a cup at the very height of triumph with the black and whites.

Moncur achieved more as a player, winning 16 full caps for Scotland and skippering his country. But, unlike Harvey, he never realised his dream of managing United despite doing steady jobs in the hot seat at Carlisle United, Hearts, Plymouth Argyle and Hartlepool.

Like Harvey before him, Moncur became an adopted Geordie living the bulk of his adult life in the North East. He'd been an outstanding schoolboy footballer playing five times for Scotland Boys at left-back or centre-half. Not unnaturally all the top clubs wanted him . . . Matt Busby at Manchester United, Stan Cullis of Wolves, and Preston North End boss Cliff Britton. The young Moncur had trials at each and every one of them but instead he turned down the great names of football to sign for the last club in the queue: Newcastle United.

'Why did I turn my back on all the glamour at the top of the tree? Because, in a nutshell, Old Trafford and Molineux lacked something that Newcastle United had in abundance: homeliness,' Bob told me. 'And that's vitally important to a kid about to go into the big wide world on his own for the first time.

'I felt like a little boy lost on my two visits to Old Trafford. The superstars were there all right but the place was cold and impersonal. My dad knew a little about Tyneside — as a laddie he had spent a few holidays at

South Shields and used to go to St. James's one week and Roker the next. United's name kept cropping up because their scout Peter Nellies was becoming persistent and dad asked if I'd like to take a look at the place. It would be the last, he said, after a summer of journeying over the Border to a string of English clubs.'

Moncur played at half-back in a practice match and, instead of returning home to Kirkliston near Edinburgh afterwards, United's boss Charlie Mitten persuaded him to stay until the Saturday.

'What foot do you kick with son?' asked Mitten.

'It's six and two threes,' replied the youngster.

'Right, you'll play at inside-left at West Wylam on Saturday.'

Moncur's response was to crack in four goals and his wanderings were over. On October 22, 1960 Bob became an apprentice professional at St. James's Park.

'This was definitely the club for me. Eveyone was so friendly and genuine. They were really interested in you as a person. Whereas before I had a feeling of just being a number, this was different. Alan Thompson, in charge of Newcastle's juniors, and team manager Ted Hughes showed an immediate interest in my progress. And to top things off two of my pals from the Scotland Boys side, John Markie and Cliff Ewington, were on the staff. I was put into digs in Whitley Bay with them. Other youngsters like David Craig, fresh over from Ireland, were just as friendly. This was great.'

The first Gallowgate milestone was little less than two years away. The Youth Cup provided the vehicle and Moncur the romance, scoring the winning goal against a club which almost signed him — Wolves — and setting a goalscoring pattern which was to be repeated in another much grander Cup final seven years later.

United had never won the Youth Cup before 1962 and they've only repeated the feat once since, incidentally. So the two-legged final against Wolves was quite an occasion.

Moncur actually couldn't get his place in United's junior

Bob Moncur, skipper of Newcastle United.

side at half-back and consequently was shoved into the attack to add a little height, weight and robustness to a smallish front line. With him in the team were other emerging stars like David Craig and Alan Suddick, a 17-year-old whose impish skills had already adorned United's League side.

A crowd of 14,000 saw United gain a creditable 1-1 draw with favourites Wolves at Molineux and 20,000 no less were in St. James's when the trophy was secured with a 1-0 scoreline. Moncur's winner was a powerful header at the near post from a Les O'Neill corner.

Bob was to become one of Britain's great sweepers, a player with such an ability to read the game, to tackle, and to intercept by anticipation that he was the bolt on United's defensive door. But early in his St. James's career he was used at inside-forward, as in the Youth Cup final, or attacking left-half. It took a senior pro, looking at a youngster battling to find a natural home in the team, to harshly bring the truth to the fore.

Stan Anderson was the king of attacking wing-halves, a player with a Rolls Royce engine in him, and he told Moncur: 'Don't be fooled into copying me, Bob. Going forward's not for you. All your strength lies in playing at the back reading the game and blocking the holes.Develop your game on those lines.'

To a headstrong youngster that was advice he didn't want to hear — glory and goals lay ahead for the adventurer — but Joe Harvey, now established as the new boss of St. James's, reiterated Anderson's words and Moncur's destiny was shaped.

Mind you, Bob crept into his first-team career rather than bludgeoned the door down. His debut as an 18-year-old at Luton Town in March, 1963 saw him sneak in a couple more games before the end of the season; three in 1963-64; 11 as United became Second Division champions in 1964-65 when a magnificent half-back line of Anderson, McGrath and Iley barred young Moncur's way; 19 in Division One in 1965-66; and 23 in 1966-67. As you can see it was slow, steady progress building towards the glory that lay ahead.

Ask Moncur all these years later to pinpoint his real breakthrough and he can do it to the very day: September 30, 1967.

'I'd almost gone to Norwich City for £25,000 during the summer and started off the new season out of the team,' recalls Bob. 'I was eventually called up against Coventry and then promptly dropped again despite us winning 3-2. I had one of my worst rows ever with the boss over that but my exile lasted a mere one game and I was back in to face Arsenal on September 30. We won a superb match 2-1 through a brilliant header by Wyn Davies in the dying

. . . and Moncur the captain of Scotland.

minutes. Wyn climbed almost as high as the pylons to head home a corner. Although I didn't realise it, I'd turned the corner at last. From that day until the end of my Newcastle career I was never dropped again.

'I played every game until the end of the season, helped United to qualify for Europe for the first time in their history, skippered the side when Jim Iley was out, and picked up Scottish caps at Under 23 and full level.'

Europe . . . ah, the memories, the magic moments, the Moncur moments. This was to be HIS season, the one every pro waits for and sometimes never gets. Robert became United's regular captain, leader of a band of players who brought European glory to a city which fell in love with the Fairs Cup. Harvey's heroes were men who wrote themselves forever into the history of the club with guts, commitment and not a little skill. It was the year of Wyn Davies, a beanpole centre-forward who terrorised the Continent with his prodigious heading power; of Pop Robson, a goalscorer supreme who was extremely unlucky never to play for England; of a little Dane called Ben Arentoft who ran continuously in the middle of the park; of the two young full-backs called David Craig and Frank Clark; and of Moncur, the rock upon which United relied and eventually a goalscorer who brought home the bacon.

By now I was on the United beat for the *Evening Chronicle* and I saw every glorious game on the way to Fairs Cup victory. The atmosphere was electric, the camaraderie first class. I remember sitting in a little bar in Estoril, a seaside resort outside Lisbon, writing my match report with Bob next to me adding quotes to highlight the story whenever I needed them. It was that sort of friendly set-up with everyone mucking in. It was a team effort off and on the park.

Bob missed the opening two-legged Fairs Cup tie against Feyenoord because of a cartilage operation when Geoff Allen, in a fleeting moment of glory before injury cruelly ended his career, carved victory at St. James's Park.

But he was back for Sporting Lisbon and the other victories against Real Zaragoza, Setubal, and Glasgow Rangers on the way to the final.

Ujpest Dozsa, who had beaten the mighty Leeds United home and away in the semi-finals, provided the last obstacle. St. James's Park was packed to capacity like a Christmas stocking about to burst at the seams for the first leg in May of 1969. Nearly 60,000 were packed inside and high above the popular side kids, arms outstretched for balance, picked their way along the roof tops risking their very lives to get a better view.

'For 63 minutes Ujpest had kept it tight at the back, slowed it down and played it around in midfield,' recalls

Moncur shows off the European Fairs Cup on United's arrival back at Newcastle Airport from a famous victory in Hungary.

Moncur. 'Possession football was the name of their game and in skipper Janoc Gorocs they had a wily old fox who excelled in such matters. We knew we had to take a decent lead to Budapest, and in an effort to get more penetration up front substitute Alan Foggon was waved onto the track to begin warming up as we won a free-kick just outside the box.

'Normally I stayed at the back but this was different. We just had to get a break. So up I went in an effort to add height and weight to our attack. Tommy Gibb lofted the free-kick to the back of the box as he so often did for big Wyn Davies. Wyn, one of the few centre-forwards who still liked to use his chest to bring a ball down, breasted it forward and as the tall Ujpest keeper Szentimihalyi came out hammered the ball against him. I could see the rebound zooming towards me as straight as a dye and I knew I must burst the net. I drew back my left foot and connected as sweet as you like.

'At that precise moment the whole world stood still for me. I had never scored a competitive goal for United's senior side and suddenly there I was in a European final engulfed by the throaty, almost hysterical roar of 60,000 Geordies.'

With Foggon on for little Jackie Sinclair, United poured forward hungry for more success.

'The ground beneath our feet almost trembled with the roar of voices which must have carried for miles on the night air. I don't know what it must have done for the Hungarians but I know what it did for us. It turned us all into giants.

'I thought I'd had my personal moment of triumph but unbelievably I scored again only 10 minutes later. Moving forward from left-half with Ujpest backing off, I played a one-two with Ben Arentoft to get within 20 or 25 yards of the goal. Suddenly the ball stood up in front of me after hitting a divot. I was about to shoot when Jim Scott ran across me. I hesitated, thinking he was going to hit it but he shouted to me to have a go and I just let fly. The ball hardly lifted as it flashed right across the box and into the far corner of the net.

'Frank Clark ran over to me as we ran back to the centre circle. "You lucky devil," he said, a grin splitting his face. "That shot must have bounced eight times before it went in." Actually it did bounce twice but it counted and that was enough for me.'

With the crowd on the verge of delirium United scored a third before the final whistle with Scott, known more for his frills than his brawn, scoring a courageous goal, toe-ending the ball over the keeper before tumbling over his prostrate body.

Davies, who took more physical hammerings than a heavyweight boxer on United's European sojourns, actually fractured his cheekbone in the match — on the back of Moncur's head. Bob, searching for his hat-trick, went into the Ujpest penalty area for another dead ball kick and when the ball was dropped short to the near post Moncur bravely stuck his head in. Davies was just a split second behind him and his cheekbone crunched into the back of Bob's head.

Malcolm Macdonald and Bob Moncur, Newcastle United's two goal-scorers, hold up the Texaco Cup they won in 1974 just before the F.A. Cup final

But it took more than a few facial injuries to keep out Wyn the Leap and he was there for the second leg behind the Iron Curtain. I've already told in the Joe Harvey chapter how United found themselves two down at the interval and on their way out only to be picked up by Harvey's rallying call. If United needed an early goal to quell the Ujpest fire, then Moncur provided it to complete an unbelievable hat-trick.

'A corner on the left saw Szentimihalyi punch out under pressure. Sinclair picked up the loose ball to return it inside the area where I was still lurking after going up for the flag kick. The ball was actually curling away from me as I swung round but I still connected with my left. From the moment my foot touched the ball I knew I had scored.

'It felt so good — like hitting a perfect iron on the golf course. The full-back standing on the line desperately tried to get a hand to the speeding ball but he had no real chance. It was the best-executed goal of my three, but to get three with my left foot wasn't bad for a right-footed player!'

Upjest's wall of invincibility had been breached. They were dead and United went on to score further goals through Arentoft and substitute Foggon to win 3-2 on the night and 6-2 on aggregate. Moncur, the unlikely hat-trick hero, lifted the Fairs Cup from FIFA president Sir Stanley Rous to complete a memorable story.

Bob is a good pal — I later ghosted his autobiography *United We Stand* — and he brought the Fairs Cup down to my home in Whitley Bay where we cavorted round the back garden with it and had our photographs taken. Carefree days!

Moncur's international career had begun in May, 1968, three months after playing against England at Hampden in an Under 23 international. He made his debut against Holland in Amsterdam and had the satisfaction of helping his country keep a clean sheet in a 0-0 draw. By his sixth international, after playing against the 'auld enemy' England in front of 134,000 at Hampden, he was captain of his country.

Skippering United and Scotland went hand-in-hand for Bob. When three successive years in Europe came to an end he captained Newcastle to success in the 1973 Anglo-Italian tournament, beating Fiorentina 2-1 in front of 45,000 screaming Italians and the following season kept up his amazing record of cup-final goals by notching one in the 2-1 Texaco Cup victory over Burnley after extra time as well as leading United to the F.A. Cup final at Wembley.

Not unnaturally the team had changed somewhat since the heady days of the Fairs Cup. If Willie McFaul, David Craig, Frank Clark and Moncur were still around in defence farther upfield, there were new faces. Terry Hibbitt was the key midfield provider with, fleetingly, Tony Green and then Tommy Cassidy, Terry McDermott and Jinky Smith. Up front were the flamboyant Malcolm Macdonald and workmanlike John Tudor.

Ironically, the Wembley final against Liverpool was to be Moncur's last game in a black and white shirt after 14 years with the club.

Bob Moncur, in cap and scarf, on the bus which took United round the town on their homecoming from the '74 Cup final. Full-back David Craig, who missed the final through injury, and goalkeeper Willie McFaul flank him.

He was sold to neighbours Sunderland for a knockdown £30,000 where he became their captain and helped them back into the First Division before embarking on a managerial career which had always looked to lie ahead of him.

At Carlisle, where he became boss in September of 1977, Moncur signed two future Newcastle stars Peter Beardsley and Neil McDonald as 'nobodies'. Bob was to make his name as a wheeler dealer in the transfer market but I doubt if he ever made a better signing than Beardsley, who was then an 18-year-old factory labourer rejected by a couple of League clubs and burning with unfulfilled ambition at Wallsend Boys Club.

'Brian Watson was my youth development officer at Brunton Park and he told me about a kid called Beardsley,' remembers Moncur. 'Peter was training with Newcastle and Brian urged me to act quickly. So we fixed it up for him to play for us in a friendly at Blue Star near Newcastle Airport. I was playing at the back and had a good look as Beardsley got our third goal in a 3-2 victory.

'I took him to the Diamond pub in Ponteland after the game — Peter didn't even drink — and asked him to sign for us. The very next night he put pen to paper in manager Billy Elliott's office at Darlington where Carlisle were playing another friendly. That miss was later to cost my old club £120,000.'

For several weeks after signing in 1979 Beardsley lived with Bob and his wife Camille as he was introduced to life in the Football League.

But by the February of the following year Moncur, feeling a change in direction was necessary, left Carlisle despite his great friendship with chairman James Bendall and headed over the Border to Hearts where he was to spend little over a year in the Scottish League. We always kept in touch — often I could help Bob with 'inside' news on players who could become available etc — but back in late 1980 I received a call with a difference. Bill McGarry had been sacked at Newcastle and Moncur wanted to know what his chances were of doing a Harvey and coming 'home'.

It was unofficial, of course, and I put the feelers out but back came the word that while Bob was extremely highly thought of in the St. James's boardroom their main target was another manager. The message was quickly relayed to Edinburgh and Moncur, ever the opportunist, asked me to help him put together a Press statement stating that he was happy at Tynecastle and had no intention of leaving.

That was the sign of the true professional . . . find out the score and then beat everyone to the punch. In lots of ways I was sad that Moncur never got to manage the club he loved above all others because he was made for them, but I quickly found out who 'the other manager' was on United's shopping list. Joe Harvey decided to use our long relation-

Skipper of a different kind — Moncur shows off the Henri Lloyd Trophy awarded to him and partner Nick Skinnard for their 'perseverance, endurance, courage and indomitable spirit' shown during the 1985 Round Britain Yacht Race.

ship by asking me to sound out Arthur Cox, who was at Chesterfield, about the vacancy. It was all on the sly, of course, but Arthur was keen, United went through the front door, and the man who was eventually to bring the likes of Keegan to Tyneside was on his way.

Moncur the traveller switched from Heart of Midlothian in Edinburgh to the south coast of England and Plymouth Argyle in the summer of 1981 for a two-year stay before, sickened by internal politics in the boardroom, he turned his back on football management to head for Tyneside. Here he bought Gateshead Squash Club and threw himself energetically into his new life.

But then Bob had always been a superb all-round sportsman. As a footballer golf was his second love and he twice won the Professional Footballers Golf Championship. He'd played a bit of bowls as a teenager too, then came squash and yachting, something he'd first dabbled in during his Edinburgh days, developed at Plymouth and brought to full bloom on Tyneside. Moncur became a highly accomplished yachtsman, completing the Round Britain and Trans Atlantic races, which is quite something.

Yachting, running a squash club and watching United play every home game meant he had an extremely busy life. But as the autumn of 1988 came round another mate of mine, Hartlepool chairman John Smart, decided to have a second go at prising Bob out of soccer retirement.

John had failed once but this time, suddenly, unexpectedly, Moncur said 'Yes'. First on a caretaker basis, then on a two-and-a-half year contract with his Fairs Cup team-mate Pop Robson as his coach.

I guess it was a challenge. Bob has always been a sucker for that!

BOB MONCUR'S RECORD

342 appearances and seven goals for United.
16 Scotland caps 1968-72 and one Under 23 cap 1968.
F.A. Youth Cup winner 1962.
Second Division championship 1965 and, with Sunderland, 1976.
European Fairs Cup winner 1969.
F.A. Cup finalist 1974.
Debut v Luton away March 30, 1963.

CHAPTER SIX

Malcolm Macdonald

Centre-forwards at Newcastle United — at least the best of them — possessed one common ingredient: the ability to excite. United have always been famous for their No. 9's . . . men of dash and verve who by tradition became folk heroes. Legends if you like. Think of Hughie Gallacher, Albert Stubbins, Jackie Milburn, Len White — and Malcolm Macdonald.

SuperMac fitted perfectly into the mould. He had everything to become a natural hero. Unquenchable speed, a thunderous shot, a scorer of spectacular goals, he led an extrovert lifestyle of champagne and cigars. There weren't many after-you-Claude Corinthian civilities in evidence when Macdonald was around, and the fans loved his bowl-'em-over type of leadership.

From 1971 until 1976 SuperMac reigned as king of Newcastle, bringing a dash of colour which lifted him and the club out of the ranks of the ordinary. It was a time when the blinds were unzipped and the sunshine came pouring in, and even if two Wembley cup-final appearances were the only concrete evidence of progress, plus two Texaco Cup wins and the Anglo-Italian Trophy, then no one felt cheated.

It was a time when SuperMac taunted, tortured and trussed up opposing defences and little men of infinite skill like Terry Hibbitt and Tony Green wove their magical patterns in midfield.

Yet Malcolm Macdonald's origins suggested little enough of what lay ahead. An average full-back at non-league Tonbridge, he was introduced to forward play with Fulham and graduated via Luton Town without ever setting foot in the First Division before Joe Harvey bought him for £180,000 in May of 1971.

Manchester United were interested but dithered: could the brash kid with the self-confidence that youth sometimes brings really do it in the top flight? Chelsea were also sniffing but it was United and Joe Harvey who took the plunge. Joe backed his own judgement as he always did and it paid off . . . though it cost him thirty thousand more than he'd expected.

Luton were in financial trouble. Vehicle and General, the insurance company of their chairman Tony Hunt, went bust and the Hatters suddenly needed some quick money. Manager Alec Stock took Macdonald to one side during training and said 'I'm going to have to sell you. You're our biggest asset and we're going to have to cash in.'

Luton were playing Cardiff the next day and had to win by two clear goals to get into next season's Watney Cup, a competition for the League's highest scorers.

'Joe Harvey of Newcastle is interested and he'll be in the stand,' Stock told his centre-forward. 'It's up to you now, you've got to do the business.' Luton won 3-0 and Malcolm — surprise, surprise — scored the lot.

Macdonald was told to report to Kenilworth Road the next morning and, after a wait of two hours during which time 'every nerve in my body was tingling', a hot and bothered Stock arrived to say: 'I've done the deal. This is the fee, this is what you'll get, and Joe Harvey is waiting for you in the Great Northern Hotel in London.' While Malcolm had been sitting nervously in the club offices Stock had driven down the M1, completed negotiations, and sped back again.

Luton's chief scout Harry Haslam, who had nurtured Macdonald since his Tonbridge days, drove him to that historic meeting outside King's Cross Station. As Malcolm walked through the door Harvey stepped forward.

'So you're the little bugger who's just cost me another £30,000,' he said. 'Sign this and sign it bloody quickly before the price goes up again.'

Malcolm Macdonald takes on the Manchester City defence in the 1976 League Cup final at Wembley.

It transpired that Stock had agreed a fee of £150,000 but overnight the price increased by £10,000 a goal! It was a shrewd piece of business by Stock but an even shrewder one by Harvey as Macdonald became the jewel in his crown.

'It was the start of a good relationship I had with Joe,' said Malcolm. 'I respected him and he believed in me. We were a good team.'

SuperMac was never a shrinking violet, and even though he was leaving the relative obscurity of Luton for soccer-mad Tyneside and the big time, he did it with the swagger of a champion instead of the apprehension of someone stepping into the unknown. He hired a sparkling new limo and persuaded a friend, complete with peaked cap, to chauffeur him to St. James's Park. When he stepped out with fans and Press men milling around, Mac got his first taste of Geordie humour.

'Hells bells,' said a voice in the crowd. 'He must be the

only player to arrive in his signing-on fee!' At that moment the bond of friendship between Geordie and player was sealed forever.

SuperMac's start wasn't particularly impressive. A 2-0 defeat at Crystal Palace was followed by a 0-0 draw with Spurs at White Hart Lane. No goals from the new boy, nor any fireworks. But wait, just wait . . .

Liverpool marked the home debut of Macdonald in front of his new fans. They were a great side as they always seem to have been. Their line-up read like a who's who of football: Clemence; Lawler, Lindsay; Smith, Lloyd, Hughes; Keegan, Thompson, Heighway, Toshack, Callaghan.

United went into battle thus: McFaul; Craig, Clark; Gibb, Burton, Moncur; Dyson, Tudor, Macdonald, Young, Hibbitt.

'I desperately wanted to score but what transpired that afternoon was beyond my wildest dreams,' recalled Malcolm. 'My first goal was a penalty to equalise at 1-1 after David Young had been brought down and then, just before half-time, I turned quickly to shoot across Ray Clemence into the top corner to give us the lead. That remained one of the best goals I ever scored and as the ball went in my old Luton saying flashed through my mind: 'Get it, turn, and shoot'. I'd based all my goalscoring on that.

'My striking partner John Tudor slipped me through the Liverpool defence for my hat-trick and from that moment the Geordie fans adopted me as SuperMac. For the rest of the game they sang 'SuperMac, superstar, how many goals have you scored so far?' The newspapers the next day were full of my new nickname and, after just two years as a striker, I was an idol.'

United beat Liverpool 3-2 but the full story isn't quite told. With just five minutes remaining, Macdonald was in full flight looking for his fourth goal when the advancing Clemence caught him full in the face with his left boot. He was carried off unconscious to a rousing reception. Exit the gladiator. Could it have been stage-managed better?

Golden goals — Malcolm Macdonald beats Burnley goalkeeper Alan Stevenson to score the first in Newcastle United's semi-final win at Hillsborough in 1974.

SuperMac simply didn't know how to stop scoring goals. In his first season he notched 30 in 52 League and Cup games (23 in 42 appearances in his first season in Division One); in 1972-73 it was 24 in 48 first team matches; in 1973-74 28 in 45 outings; and in 1974-75, 32 goals in 58 starts. That was his last season under his greatest ally, Joe Harvey, and even though new boss Gordon Lee made a habit of downgrading SuperMac, preferring the much more pedestrian Alan Gowling, he still managed 24 goals from 56 games in 1975-76.

During that time SuperMac made two Wembley appearances in the 1974 F.A. Cup Final against Liverpool and the 1976 League Cup final against Manchester City as well as helping United win the Texaco Cup twice and the Anglo-Italian Trophy though he couldn't play in the final in Florence after scoring a hat-trick in the semis because he was on England duty.

SuperMac and I became firm friends. He was my type of player and my type of person. We knocked around together enjoying many a jar and a good laugh. Life was for living and we did it with a certain abandonment.

Once we employed Malcolm and another old mate of

mine, Rodney Bewes, he of *The Likely Lads* fame, to shoot a couple of TV adverts for the *Chronicle.* The shooting was to take place on the Sunday morning in London after United had played at Ipswich on the Saturday. Naturally to us that meant a good night on the town. Rodney, ever the pro, wouldn't join us so Malcolm and I did as much as possible to make up for the disappointment!

Come the next morning we were like two drowned rats while the nauseatingly healthy Bewes was jumping around bright and breezy. To make matters worse the director decided to film the news ads featuring Bewes first and we sat around from 10am until 4pm, at which time Malcolm and I were called for the soccer ad. No one could find us . . . until the floor manager walked behind a piece of scenery and discovered his two potential TV stars stretched out fast asleep and snoring like babies.

He must have thought we were completely nerveless for rookies, but I can assure you there's only one thing more powerful than nerves, and that's the oncoming of sleep. I don't know if it was the fear of failure or sheer exhaustion returning by the second, but we got our little scene cracked in two takes and were on our way north happily snoozing on the train. What's more, the ads were part of one of the most successful TV campaigns ever run by the *Chron.*

While SuperMac was essentially the funster, there was a serious side to him as well. A side I saw — and appreciated — more than once. I used to ghost Malcolm's column in the *Evening Chronicle* every Monday, and just before one season opened we arranged to meet at the Swallow Hotel in the centre of town on the Saturday lunchtime after training. I'd just lost my son Nicky at 11 weeks old and was naturally devastated. When I turned up, Malcolm was already sitting in the restaurant. We had our meal, did the column, and settled down to enjoy our coffee and cigars. I thought the wine waiter was a bit attentive and the bottle never seemed to empty. He'd been primed by Malcolm to slide another into the ice bucket without a fuss whenever

SuperMac is congratulated by his striking partner John Tudor on the final whistle at Hillsborough.

necessary as we talked and talked about anything and everything. Mal knew I needed to relax from the pressures of a week living in Shotley Bridge Hospital with Nicky and, like a good pal, he was ready to help without making a fuss.

That lunch went on until 10 o'clock at night before I ordered a taxi and went off home. Malcolm, God bless him, had given up his whole day. You don't forget things like that.

The column, incidentally, was dynamic. Footballers' ghosted columns can easily be nondescript with them unwilling to go out on a limb: you know the sort of thing — we played well last Saturday but didn't have any luck — but being SuperMac he was never afraid to speak his mind in public. Everyone came in for a slagging if he thought it was justified — the League, the Football Association, the lot. I remember one day after Gordon Lee had arrived, the back page lead carried the headline 'Lee gags his players', and above it was Macdonald's column as frank and fearless as ever!

SuperMac scored a basketful of spectacular goals in a black and white shirt but the abiding memory for me was on the run to the F.A. Cup final in 1974. He took some stick nationally for not scoring in the final against Liverpool but, to be honest, United never got over the halfway line that day and folk seemed to quickly forget that it was Macdonald who had been mainly responsible for Newcastle getting there in the first place.

He scored in every round away from home — at Watford against Hendon, at Scunthorpe, West Bromwich Albion, and Nottingham Forest at Goodison, before topping it all off with two of the most clinical goals of his career to defeat Burnley 2-0 in the semi-final at Hillsborough.

Just to underline that the height of his career was spent on Tyneside, Macdonald gained all his 14 England caps (and his four Under 23 caps for that matter) while with United. He never really saw himself as an international striker where subtlety and a deft touch was required, but

One of SuperMac's greatest ever goals for United. He strikes a magnificent right-foot shot into the net at Bolton in the fifth round of the F.A. Cup in 1976.

more of an old-fashioned leader of the line at club level. That's as maybe but, apart from scoring against world champions West Germany, SuperMac had one great moment in the white shirt of his country — and I was privileged to be there to see it.

England were playing Cyprus at Wembley in 1975 and just before the kick-off Brian Glanville of the *Sunday Times* was at great pains to point out to me why SuperMac was never a true international. Well, the game got under way and Malcolm scored one, two, three, four, FIVE goals to equal the individual scoring record for England. He knocked in every solitary England goal that night, and if a slow smile became wider and wider with every strike adding to Glanville's discomfort, then I couldn't help it. SuperMac had the last laugh as usual.

What Malcolm didn't realise at the time was that his Newcastle honeymoon was about to end. Joe Harvey quit as manager, and in his place United appointed a brash young manager, Gordon Lee, who hated the star system.

This is how SuperMac later described his introduction to Lee in his autobiography:

'Gordon Lee didn't like me even before he came to Newcastle. I was in South Africa when he was appointed manager in the summer of 1975. I'd been doing a weekly column for the *Evening Chronicle* and John Gibson, a good friend of mine, telephoned me with the news.

'The new manager's been appointed,' he said. 'Who do you think?'

'Cloughie,' I said.

'No.'

'Jack Charlton.'

'No.'

'Lawrie McMenemy.'

'No.'

'Don't tell me they've given it to Bob Stokoe,' I said.

'No.'

Christ,' I said. 'I'm running short of ideas. Go on, I give in.'

'Gordon Lee.'

'Gordon who?' I said. I'd never heard of him. John went on to explain that Lee had steered Blackburn to promotion from the Third Division and that he was a strict disciplinarian. 'He was appointed yesterday,' John added, 'and this morning there's a piece in all the daily newspapers in which he's slagged you off for appearing in a beer advert.'

'There was a brand of beer called Tartan Bitter and I'd agreed to endorse it with other players such as Roy McFarland and Dave Mackay. All it involved was a picture of me on the advert and McTartan Bitter underneath. Now it's common knowledge that players like a glass of beer after a match and I couldn't see any harm in it, nor could I see any harm in publicly associating myself with it. Gordon Lee thought otherwise. It seemed that he felt I should be brought to heel and that my face should not appear on beer adverts.

'There was more to come. Apparently Lee had said, 'I will have no stars in my team', and when the Press lads asked who he was referring to he replied, 'You know who it is'. Eventually someone asked, 'Are you referring to

Malcolm Macdonald and author John Gibson pictured during the making of a TV commercial to advertise the *Evening Chronicle*.

Malcolm Macdonald?' and Lee said, 'If that's what you think, well yes.' 'Our relationship just went from bad to worse.'

Lee loved his 'thinking footballers', men like Alan Gowling, Geoff Nulty, Micky Burns and Graham Oates who used to sit doing the *Daily Telegraph* crossword. He hated Jack the Lads such as SuperMac. 'My inherited boozers,' he once called them.

Gowling, an ambling, ungainly striker, was a favourite and Lee often would boost him at the expense of SuperMac. One day at Stoke, Lee held an after-match Press conference and announced: 'I've the best centre-forward in the country here. He should be playing for England in every match.'

The national newspaper men thought he was referring to Macdonald until he added: 'And didn't he score a good goal today?' Mac hadn't been on the mark and Gowling had. It caused a few open mouths, I can tell you.

By the end of season 1975-76 after SuperMac had played at Wembley in the League Cup final, the break was complete. Lee and Macdonald were poles apart and United's greatest hero was sold off to Arsenal for

£333,333. Mac departed in the same style he arrived — this time by a private chartered plane — but as always he had the last word.

United were going well the next season and were lying third top when they went to Highbury at the beginning of December. They were cut down 5-3 in a spectacular game on an icy surface and SuperMac scored three of the Arsenal goals. And in the return at the end of April Macdonald scored again at St. James's Park as Arsenal completed the double 2-0.

However, Malcolm's career back home in London was blighted by knee injuries which finally ended his playing career at the young age of 29. He played in the 1978 Cup final when Arsenal lost 1-0 to Ipswich but could hardly run and had a cartilage removed two days after Wembley. When they went back the following year — and won 3-2 against Manchester United — Mac was recovering from a second op on a knee.

He finally bowed to the inevitable on August 3, 1979 and was quickly appointed commercial manager at one of his old clubs, Fulham. A year later he was their manager after Bobby Campbell was sacked and a new, exciting career seemed to open before him as he expertly piloted Fulham from near the bottom of the Third Division to within a point of the First.

Macdonald had some great young players. He signed Ray Houghton from West Ham on a free transfer — the same player who went on to fame with Liverpool and Eire. He also brought through Dean Coney, Gordon Davies and Paul Parker, later to get into the England squad as a QPR defender.

But tragedy lay ahead. Malcolm resigned as Fulham's manager for personal reasons — he had fallen in love with a girl called Nicky Thompson, and soccer's directors couldn't live with the fact that he left home and five daughters for her. He was shunned by the game and went off to Worthing to run a pub appropriately called the Far Post. It was a difficult time — I knew and liked his first wife

SuperMac as the United fans remember him. He signals yet another goal with Leeds United's keeper David Harvey on the floor and defender Paul Reaney also well beaten.

Julie, and as a friend who stood by him I was invited to his wedding when he and Nicky tied the knot.

Macdonald dabbled in football through newspaper columns and an agency which led directly to United's historic signing of Brazilian international Mirandinha before — respectable again — he was appointed manager of Huddersfield Town. That was to be a bitter sweet experience and sadly short. He inherited a bad team, felt he couldn't turn things round under the financial restrictions imposed on him, and resigned within a matter of months.

Under such circumstances it was perhaps not surprising that he turned back to the people who had loved him so much, buying a hotel at Berwick on the banks of the beautiful River Tweed.

Malcolm Ian Macdonald was back 'home' in the North East.

MALCOLM MACDONALD'S RECORD

227 appearances for United, scoring 121 goals. His Football League record as a goalscorer was five in 13 games for Fulham, 49 in 88 for Luton Town, 95 in 187 for Newcastle, and 42 in 84 for Arsenal.
14 England caps 1972-76 and four Under 23 caps 1972-73. One Football League appearance 1972.
F.A. Cup final appearances 1974 with United and 1978 with Arsenal.
League Cup final appearance with United 1976.
Equalled the individual scoring record for England with five goals against Cyprus at Wembley in 1975.
Debut v Crystal Palace away August 14, 1971.

CHAPTER SEVEN

Kevin Keegan

He was hailed by Stan Seymour as 'the greatest signing this club has ever made'. He was a colossus who stood only 5ft 8in tall in his stockinged feet. And he was the inspiration behind a Newcastle United revival that took them from the realms of Second Division also-rans back into Division One with style and panache in two short years.

Yet Kevin Keegan always said he was sad that the loyal United fans never saw him at the very pinnacle of his career. It was true that Keegan had won every one of his honours before arriving on Tyneside on that historic day, August 19, 1982. He had collected 63 international caps for England, culminating in his being made captain, had won the First Division championship three times with Liverpool plus the F.A. Cup and the European Cup and been voted Footballer of the Year in 1976. Then, off to Hamburg, and the honours continued to pour in — West German Man of the Year 1978, European Footballer of the Year 1978 and 1979, the Bundesliga championship 1979 and a second European Cup final.

He was a genuine superstar who, in his own eyes, may have been on the other side of the hill when he joined United but, my oh my, what a lot he gave to Tyneside in those two memorable seasons! There may have been no medal at the end of it but almost single-handedly he shook a sleeping giant into life and gave back to everyone with a black and white heart what they craved above all else: their pride.

Certainly his arrival had all the impact of a runaway train hitting the buffers. It shook the world of football to its very foundations. Here was the current England captain forsaking the First Division at Southampton for the backwaters of Division Two and a club which had a historic past but apparently little future. United at the time were going nowhere fast and manager Arthur Cox knew it. He desperately needed a personality to spark a revival and had dared to go for the very best.

It was an inspirational signing, a single piece of business which was to transform the stature of Cox and establish him as one of the best-loved managers of recent years in the eyes of United's supporters.

Keegan, already a millionaire, was a man who lived for challenges, and thereby lay the key to United's success. The genteel atmosphere of soccer on the south coast at Southampton was beginning to lose its appeal and the thought of returning to a footballing hotbed which needed a player like Keegan to lift it was tempting to the little man. Kevin, a shrewd manipulator behind his carefully constructed public image, had been wise enough to insert a clause in his Southampton contract when he returned from West Germany fixing any future transfer fee at £100,000. That meant he was well within United's financial grasp and only his wages presented an obstacle. United, to their credit, came up with the perfect answer. They wheeled in their main sponsors, Scottish and Newcastle Breweries, to offer Keegan a promotional job on the side which would top up his money to a significant degree. They even took S & N officials with them to a secret meeting with KK in London, three days before he signed, to outline their ambitious plans.

In the meantime Newcastle's interest in Keegan had hit the newspapers. He was also being linked with Manchester United, and Tyneside's reaction was a loud belly laugh. There was no way in their eyes the England skipper was going to come here instead of Old Trafford. It was merely another publicity stunt.

Within the *Evening Chronicle* we were buzzing with anticipation. We knew the Keegan interest was genuine but United, anxious not to cause waves at a delicate stage

A chilly looking Kevin Keegan arriving at Newcastle Airport on his way to sign for Newcastle United in 1982.

of negotiations, wouldn't stand up the story with quotes. We desperately needed a breakthrough. Often on these occasions it comes through old contacts — people a newspaperman knows in the game who are willing to give a tip-off on the back of friendship. And so it was to prove here.

Kevin was committed to play for Southampton against Utrecht in Holland and had to fly out to rejoin his club's pre-season tour. The Saints had been guaranteed £15,000 for the game but only if the England captain was in their side.

Match over, it was decision day — and I was sitting hundreds of miles away across the North Sea without a firm break on the biggest news story in quite a while. The front page was cleared in anticipation but nobody was saying owt and the clock was ticking away relentlessly towards my deadline. There was only one thing to do — try and contact Southampton boss Lawrie McMenemy at his hotel. Now that's easier said than done when it comes to Continental phone calls. After much to-ing and fro-ing, the nearest I got to Lawrie was John Mortimore, his No. 2. It seemed the whole world was chasing the Big Man and John was his buffer. He listened sympathetically but explained he couldn't say a word. Those were instructions. Another idea bites the dust. . .

I was preparing a speculation piece when the phone rang on my desk 10 minutes before edition time and about an hour after my negative conversation with Mortimore. Damn it, I thought, another interruption.

'Hello.'

'John, it's Lawrie McMenemy.'

'Who?'

'Lawrie. Listen mate, I haven't got much time. Keegan is flying direct to Newcastle on the British Caledonian flight. His plane will arrive at ten to twelve. Be there — Newcastle are planning a Press conference at the Gosforth Park Hotel tonight.'

As Lawrie talked he was constantly interrupted by the beep, beep, beep from the coin box quickly followed by the sound of gilders being fed in to keep us connected. He was phoning from Amsterdam Airport before he and the rest of the Southampton party boarded one plane for the south coast and Keegan another for Tyneside. There was very little time, and the nuisance of trying to work foreign coin boxes must have been offputting, but Lawrie, bless him, knew I was in trouble and pulled me out. That's friendship — we'd grown up together in footballing terms when I was a cub reporter covering non-league Gateshead many, many moons before and he was their fresh-faced young coach, and we'd never lost touch.

As a direct result of Lawrie's call I met the plane, carried an all-editions page-one story including airport photo-

Keegan, with manager Arthur Cox in attendance, signs on the dotted line.

photograph of a chilled Keegan stoppping onto Tyneside, and attended the evening Press conference safe in the knowledge that we'd been 'on the ball'.

Such was the public reaction to Keegan's arrival that I wouldn't have been at all surprised had he walked on the River Tyne. He was, in the eyes of the North East, a miracle worker no less, but in a team game it isn't as simple as that, of course. He may have been the lynchpin, the inspiration, but he needed physical and skilful support to bring about a lasting improvement. That support took a year to put together but it came totally because of his presence.

Though Keegan's first season was one of appraisal as the springboard was built, the man himself got off to the magical start his stature demanded. QPR were the bit players and there was a capacity house of 36,000 to witness the grand entrance. There was only one goal in it but — naturally — it was KK who got it, rifling the ball home at the Gallowgate end to be swallowed up by wildly cheering fans.

A little man, heavily muscled with tight curly hair and a pleasing smile, Keegan's image was strictly clean-cut but shrewdly manipulated by a master who knew precisely how to drain every ounce of public acclaim from any given situation. That's not meant as a criticism, merely a statement of fact. Keegan was the ultimate PR man.

His contract with Scottish and Newcastle Breweries underlined his abilities as a manipulator. There was no question of teetotal Keegan being pictured with a pint in his hand, but he didn't see working for a brewery as contradicting his lifestyle. His was community work, meeting customers, presenting prizes and working on a series of Sunday coaching courses with schoolchildren at United's Benwell training ground.

Part of his workload involved an S & N Road Show to go round their top pubs and clubs, and I was roped in to do the stage work with KK. It was nothing new to me — I'd done talk-ins for years with a host of international celebrities — but Keegan was in a class apart. I'd seen adulation at first hand . . . for Geoff Boycott days after completing his 100th

The master and his apprentice — Kevin Keegan and Peter Beardsley.

hundred and Australian pace bowler Dennis Lillee on a tour of England at the very height of his career. But Keegan topped the lot.

Week after week he filled the pubs and clubs of Tyneside to bursting point. He was like the Pied Piper: everyone followed. He generated the electric atmosphere of a pop star with my voice inevitably drowned in a storm of welcome at the very mention of his name. On he would bound, a little man with the angelic smile of the Mona Lisa to captivate every man jack with his wit and patter. The show would last from 8pm until nearly 11 o'clock with only a 20-minute break — and then there would be a marathon autograph session!

Keegan would sit down at the front of the stage and order everyone into an orderly queue before beginning a ritual which would never alter. He wouldn't just sign his name. It was personally inscribed: he would pose happily for a photograph and would chat away for minutes at a time with each and every fan. The time would tick, tick away; committee men would look anxiously at their watches thinking longingly of bed, but still Keegan would be at it. Midnight would pass every solitary show we did before, everyone satisfied, Kevin would be ready to call it a night.

Keegan's charisma drew people round him like bees round a honey pot. Not only fans but established internationals wanted to play with a man who was one of the game's greats. Terry McDermott, once such a promising a player at Newcastle, arrived from Liverpool where he had been a European Cup winner and an England international, and David McCreery, very much part of Northern Ireland's fairytale World Cup exploits in Spain, came from America. Fleetingly, too, we saw the skills of Keegan's old mate Mike Channon and a Liverpool reserve striker Howard Gayle on loan, but overall United weren't ready for promotion. In Keegan's first season they finished fifth in Division Two with their top player scoring 21 League goals in 37 appearances, enough to see him deservedly crowned the North East's Player of the Year at a lavish awards ceremony run by my newspaper and our sponsors Hennessy Cognac.

KK loved Arthur Cox. They had a father and son relationship much like the one he had enjoyed at Liverpool with the legendary Bill Shankly.

But the little fella was strong-willed. He was bigger than the club if you like, and with time running out on his glittering career, failure was something he wasn't going to accept at this late stage. It was abhorrent to him.

He'd arrived on a one-year contract, and if his stay was to be extended, then it was to be because success was just round the corner. His thoughts were revealed in an exclusive interview I did with him in April when he stated bluntly that if Arthur Cox left, he'd go too. He added that he wanted United to buy class players before he would commit himself to a new contract for the following season.

'I'm not holding a gun to their head but I want to see some movement from the club,' Keegan told me. 'I want to

K.K. in the famous black and white stripes with Chris Waddle.

play with a better all-round squad next season so that we can gain more success. It's as much for the benefit of the fans as for myself. They deserve so much after all this time.

'I joined Newcastle because I've always put my faith in people not bricks and mortar, and neither Arthur Cox nor Stan Seymour have let me down. But at this stage of my career I don't want failure.'

They were chilling words cutting through the euphoria he had created on the terraces, but they refelected the man himself — outspoken, committed, and hungry to be a winner. Cox called him unique, and it was certainly a unique deal that Keegan eventually signed. His new deal had clauses which allowed him to bail out at Christmas for a transfer fee of £75,000. If he went between Christmas and the end of the season, the fee would be £50,000; and at the end of the season he would get a free.

If it was meant as a kick up the backside to those upstairs — a safety net against any growing lack of ambition with Keegan safely signed up — then it worked. Cox was allowed to buy, and before a ball was kicked in anger he signed goalkeeper Martin Thomas permanently and brought in two new full-backs, Malcolm Brown and John Ryan, for a joint outlay of £325,000. But it was an outgoing transfer which rocked Tyneside. Keegan's strike partner Ray Varadi, much against his wishes, was sold to promotion rivals Sheffield Wednesday. Varadi had scored 42 goals in two seasons, and that was enough to ingratiate him with the fans, but not Keegan.

I well remember a do at the Supporters' Club in the couple of days the transfer was on the boil. Varadi was almost in tears at the thought of leaving, and the supporters to a man were behind him. But Cox knew what the fans didn't — Varadi wasn't the perfect foil for Kevin.

Keegan, having played at the very top of his profession, liked to link with someone who had a good first touch and could play quick one-twos to put one of them within striking range. Varadi, on the other hand, was not a touch

Keegan, covered in black and white momentoes, waves goodbye to the fans with promotion from the Second Division clinched.

player and preferred the ball played over the top so that he could use his lightning pace. In those circumstances only one player was going to go.

Maybe that's player power but the outcome was to guarantee United promotion. Peter Beardsley, who possessed the caress of a velvet glove, was imported from Vancouver Whitecaps, and with Chris Waddle having shrugged off the apprehension of playing with a superstar (something which blighted his early days under Keegan), the three of them became a potent force up front. Each was an artist in his own right, two youngsters blossoming at the knee of the golden oldie.

United, having shrugged off the shackles of self-doubt, blossomed in the autumn sunshine of Keegan's career. By the time October came round, six successive League victories had them into a gallop and, with central defender Glenn Roeder from QPR aboard, the New Year arrived to a similar harvest. One game was lost in February and none the following month.

Keegan knew what we didn't — that he was about to retire — and he announced it with typical showmanship. On his 33rd birthday, St. Valentine's Day, 1984, slap bang in the middle of United's promotion surge, the headlines blared: 'Keegan Quits Soccer'. He was to call it a day at the end of the season and he wanted the black and white faithful to know that he would never kick a ball for any other club. It worked like a charm: the final bond had been forged. Only promotion, Keegan's farewell present to Tyneside, needed to be achieved.

And it was. On Easter Monday poor Carlisle United were swept aside 5-1 in front of 33,386 with Keegan and Waddle scoring twice and Beardsley knocking in the other goal. In the next home game the gate was bumped up to 35,850 as Derby County were clinically taken apart 4-0 with the same talented trio responsible, and two days later a 2-2 draw at Huddersfield clinched promotion.

The finale was against Brighton at St. James's and it was sheer theatre. United were up and their god was saying

Keegan shakes hands with the faithful on his lap of honour.

goodbye. A full house of 36,145 packed the ground to witness the very last Football League appearance of one of the game's greats and, my, he didn't disappoint one of them. United won 3-1 and KK scored in his last match just as he had in his first for United.

But stars always take a second curtain call and Keegan's old club Liverpool were brought to the park for a nostalgic send-off which saw the great man lifted from the centre circle by helicopter on the final whistle. It was a bigger weepie than ET's Hollywood lift-off in the flying saucer!

Keegan was, of course, United's top gun in the promotion season, scoring 27 League goals in 41 appearances, seven more than Beardsley and nine more than Waddle.

Sadly for me, there was a bittersweet ending to the Keegan days. He publicly came out against a book I had written (with his permission) on his lifestory. I can't pretend I wasn't deeply wounded and confused. There seemed no apparent reason for it, but I found out much later that, by accident, my book was to hit the market before the official club brochure marking his retirement and was therefore likely to cream the market before the club could cash in. It was political — I was in the way — but I found it hard to take after the friendship I had forged working with him on the S & N Road Shows. If only someone had spoken with me instead of making a public stand, I could have come to some financial agreement with United.

But to hell with it. Keegan was one of the most inspiring players ever to pull on a black and white shirt, and my lasting memories are all good ones. Like thousands of Geordies, I'm eternally grateful that Kevin came into our lives and touched us all in his special way.

It was short but oh so sweet.

KEVIN KEEGAN'S RECORD

85 games for United and 49 goals (78 League games for 48 goals).
First Division championships with Liverpool: 1972-73, 1975-76, 1976-77.
Bundesliga championship with Hamburg: 1979.
UEFA Cup winner with Liverpool 1972-73, 1975-76.
European Cup winner with Liverpool: 1976-77. Finalist with Hamburg: 1979-80.
F.A. Cup winner with Liverpool: 1973-74 (against United).
English Footballer of the Year: 1976.

West German Man of the Year: 1978.
European Footballer of the Year: 1978, 1979.
English PFA Footballer of the Year: 1982.
North East Footballer of the Year with United: 1983, 1984.
England career: 63 caps, 21 goals. Five Under 23 caps.

CHAPTER EIGHT

Chris Waddle

Ugly ducklings can grow up into graceful swans. Here is living proof if any were ever needed. Waddle was an ungainly footballer in his youth. He ran with shoulders hunched as though carrying a sack of coal on his back. Nay, trundled rather than ran. Head down, arms flapping, lackadaisical, he frustrated managers and coaches alike who could see talent without being able to reach deep inside to the rich vein beneath the surface.

But as years added the supreme confidence of an athlete who knows his special capabilities Waddle became an artist. Put a football in his path and he glided, swaying mesmerisingly to taunt and unbalance his opponent, before effortlessly moving away. One moment he was there, the next . . . whoosh, he was gone! They knew what he was going to do, it was simply that they couldn't stop him.

Waddle, like the great Wor Jackie, like SuperMac, like his contemporary Beardsley, was not blessed with the education of a Football League club from the day he first discarded his school satchel. Oh sure, clubs had watched the painfully shy, small schoolboy from Heworth Grange. He'd even gone ever so fleetingly to Newcastle United for twice a week training as a 13-year-old in 1974 and had a spell with Coventry City where homesickness became chronic but as a 16-year-old he signed on the dole, receiving the princely sum of £10 30p.

A job as a sausage seasoner relieved Waddle of that particular hell of the dole queue but football was still no more than flirtation rather than a way of life.

My earliest meeting with Chris was, strangely, something he remembered and I didn't! Mind you, there was a

Chris Waddle neatly takes the ball away from a defender.

good reason for that — it was long before he became a household name, when even I was actually more in the public eye than him, at least on Tyneside. Waddle was playing for Clarke Chapmans, and being the local sports editor I annually presented their end-of-season awards, taking along one of the United players to add a bit of sparkle. This particular night I was with John Connolly, who possessed the roguish humour which often blesses the Scots, and we duly handed over the trophies to a succession of kids, had photographs taken, and downed a few lagers. It was pleasant but I thought nothing of it particularly. It was merely another night of prizegiving like many I endured, and still do, as part of my job. It was only years later that Chris pulled me and produced a slightly tattered photograph of the Clarke Chapmans team group with Connolly and me in the back row.

He pointed to a youngster in the front row. It was a very young Chris Waddle, long before he became an England international. I remember a similar incident with Steve Cram, the athlete who later became the Commonwealth, European and World 1,500 metres champion and often wonder how many more faceless kids who have received a quick handshake and trophy have gone on to greater things.

Waddle was confined to playing on the infamous sloping pitch of Tow Law in the Drybroughs Northern League before United at last introduced him to the full-time game in the summer of 1980. Former England striker Allan Clarke had offered him a trial at Barnsley, which he turned down, and Sunderland, the club he had supported as a boy, took him for a short stay only for Ken Knighton and Frank Clark to tell him he was no better than what they already had, a decision which came back to haunt them.

United were in the hinterlands of the Second Division when Waddle arrived and, within a blink of an eyelid, manager Bill McGarry was sacked. The man who took over, Arthur Cox, was to coax, cajole and even bully Chris into becoming an international. The learning years were hard inasmuch as whenever there seemed a lull in events Press-wise Cox would always appear to have a go at Waddle but it was his way of giving a talented youngster a kick up the backside. No ability was to be wasted if Cox had anything to do with it.

Waddle made his Football League debut in that first season, against Shrewsbury at St. James's Park. It was in midweek, the rain sleeted down all night, and Shrewsbury were typically difficult to play against. A Bobby Shinton goal made it a winning start but while the promise was there it was a competent performance rather than a spectacular one.

Chris was still the introvert rather than the brash kid Paul Gascoigne was from day one. He took the 59 bus to the ground, as he did for quite a while on match days, and wore a fifteen quid suit he had picked up in the sales. Often

The Waddler skips round Sheffield Wednesday defenders Peter Shirtliff and Gary Megson.

as his career began to unfold Waddle would slip onto the back seat of the bus upstairs and bury himself in The Pink so as he wouldn't be recognised by the fans. He'd listen as the banter went on about the match without ever daring to join in.

That first season Waddle played a total of 17 League and Cup games, scoring three goals. It was enough to win himself a two-year contract at £120 a week basic plus £70 appearance money, not a fortune by any means but a welcome step in the right direction especially as he was to play in all 47 matches during the 1981-82 campaign.

Such a run, during which time glimpses of the Waddle of tomorrow began to emerge, brought tangible results. He still had a year of his old contract remaining but Cox, encouraged by the lanky lad with a knack of doing the unexpected, bumped up his wage packet to £415 a week and he was promised a car if he scored 20 goals. The Football League player who couldn't drive and got a bus to the match had been a good story for the nationals but it took Chris no fewer than four tests to get his licence — just in case!

Before the 1982-83 season started United went on a trip to Madeira during which time the coach Tommy Cavanagh, who used to be Tommy Docherty's sidekick at Manchester United, got the players together to announce: 'We've signed Keegan.' First reaction was one of disbelief, even to scoff at such outrageous suggestions. But the team returned to Keegan mania. Cox had brought off the signing of a lifetime and the joyride was about to begin.

For a young local player like Waddle it was all too much. The initial promise was engulfed in the barrage of headlines and national coverage which heralded Keegan's arrival on Tyneside. His form dipped under the weight of new-found pressure and he went out of the team. Transfer speculation took over. A swap deal with Brighton, another with Portsmouth involving Kevin Dillon and a third with Tony Henry of Bolton put a question mark over his future.

Keegan's answer was direct — Waddle wasn't fit enough. 'I can understand it,' said Cox. 'Waddle missed the formative years for a soccer pro between 15 and 19. Consequently he has had too much to catch up with in the professional game. He almost went to pieces at the start of the season when Kevin set Tyneside alight. Waddle just froze in the big crowd atmosphere.'

Waddle's unathletic appearance when he was not on the ball made him look unfit. He wasn't a sleek machine, he looked wrong when others were in possession. But he suffered from more than that. He was still basically shy despite his limited success — I always remember in those days Chris would prefer to stay in the dressing-room after a game rather than walk down a crowded corridor and face the inevitable barrage of questions.

Cox's job was to harness the player's talents to his real potential. Chris had to win not only the battle on the field

Waddle pictured at Newcastle Airport with manager Arthur Cox holding the Japan Cup United won on their Kevin Keegan tour of 1983.

but in his head as well. To achieve it Cox adopted a mixture of encouragement, discipline, bullying and competition. If the moment was right the boss would have a go. Long after Arthur departed John Anderson, a free transfer signing from Preston who became one of United's most dependable stars, told me: 'I hated that man at the time. But now I realise just how much he did for my career.' Waddle was to feel much the same way.

Chris got back in the side during October and in his third comeback game against Burnley scored the sort of goal which was to become his trademark. He received the ball wide in their half and ran across the pitch, cut into the centre beating a couple of players, and struck a thunderous 30-yard shot past an unmoving Alan Stevenson into the top corner. Those moments made all the persistence worthwhile.

Like a lot of young players Waddle's form hit peaks and troughs though he was to stay in the team. Keegan's first season ended with Chris playing a respectable 40 League and Cup games, scoring seven goals but, much more important, winning the battle within himself.

Confidence was something which he had to acquire the hard way but now, like an overcoat in the first throws of summer, self-doubt was discarded forever. Marriage to Lorna, the arrival of Peter Beardsley, and the fact that goals breed belief combined to produce a player on the very top of his form. The swan had replaced the ugly duckling.

In the opening game of what was to become the promotion season Waddle even ended up in goal at Leeds. Anderson had given United the lead when early in the second half Kevin Carr came out for a cross and fell heavily on his elbow. Keegan offered to go in goal and so, unexpectedly, did Waddle. Cox, perhaps afraid that the smallish Keegan could get chipped, agreed that it should be Chris, but when he tried to pull the jersey off Carr he screamed in agony. His arm was broken.

Amazingly Waddle kept a clean sheet and United won 1-0 to begin their points haul. But it wasn't Chris the goal stopper but the goal scorer — and maker — who propelled United towards the First Division.

Keegan, Waddle and Beardsley were a front line which possessed everything . . . skill, vision, creativity and finishing power. It was First Division quality playing in the Second. How I loved to watch them play, creating intricate patterns and then cutting direct into the heart of the opposition. Each a star in his own right.

Waddle's final figures were an ever-present 42 outings for 18 goals which equalled his total over the previous three seasons.

What we didn't foresee, of course, was the disintegration which was to follow. Keegan's impending retirement had been announced but Waddle was to follow a season later, leaving on freedom of contract, and Beardsley was to walk out shortly afterwards. Their departures were to anger and sicken the Geordie fans and I don't blame them for one moment.

Cox, who had so much to do with the development of Waddle, left on a contractual dispute during the summer

Chris Waddle when he was voted North East Player of the Year. Left to right are Maurice Hennessy of sponsors Hennessy Cognac, Waddle, Sunderland goalkeeper Chris Turner who was third, runner-up Peter Beardsley, England manager Bobby Robson and author John Gibson.

and the manager who was to follow him, Jack Charlton, was very much a different animal. Cox had gone for imagination and flair whereas Big Jack liked the long ball game . . . 'playing one-twos with God' as he put it. His style wasn't going to suit Waddle or Beardsley who liked the ball played to feet, creating through personal ability.

Charlton's man management was brusque. He was insensitive, not knowing players' names nor bothering himself too much to find them out. Waddle and Beardsley became 'big un' and 'little un', Neil McDonald was frequently referred to as Gary Macdonald, a centre-forward he had at Middlesbrough; and young keeper Gary Kelly became Chris after the TV personality!

It was all hard to take, especially for Waddle and Beardsley, but the early results papered over the cracks. United got off to a flyer in Division One with three successive wins, but while that was later to be put into perspective, Waddle's standards never slipped.

He was, simply, brilliant. My undying memory is of Chris in that third game against Aston Villa. He scored twice and made the other for Beardsley in a 3-0 victory. Roaming up front, he would explode with devastating effect.

Villa had absolutely no answer. But then, neither would anyone else with Waddle in that mood. Yet he had gone into the game having received an early morning call from his brother Ray telling him his dad had suffered a stroke.

A short time later Waddle surpassed even his Villa performance. On Queen's Park Rangers' artificial pitch he was inspirational. United, unbelievably, led 4-0 at half-time but even more unbelievably were pegged back to 5-5 at the end of an exhausting 90 minutes. Chris had scored a hat-trick and made another goal in front of an admiring England boss Bobby Robson and his international career was assured.

The first step came when Waddle was picked as an over-age player in England's Under 21 squad against Finland, only four years after leaving Tow Law. The game was at Southampton and within two minutes he had scored, helping his country to win 2-0. Chris was now at the very zenith of his career with United, a player of poise, dash and flair. Yet away from the arena that shy trait still lingered just beneath the surface.

He was now much in demand on Tyneside — a celebrity. Whenever I was approached about talk-ins the name of Waddle kept cropping up. The public wanted to meet their hero. I knew Chris's agent, Alistair Garvie, very well. He'd been United's assistant secretary and had left to open his own business handling Waddle, Paul Gascoigne and a host of cricketers. What about the Waddler doing chat shows? We thought we'd give it a try.

I've often mused that footballers are peculiar animals. They can play in front of 50,000 without turning a hair but put them in front of 300 folk with a microphone in their hand and a lot of them become nervous wrecks. There are exceptions — Keegan, Glenn Roeder, Paul Goddard and Gazza were value for money. But Peter Beardsley, good

Waddle the pop star — the publicity pictures for his hit single 'Diamond Lights' with Spurs team-mate Glenn Hoddle.

little player that he was, never appeared comfortable as a Geordie Terry Wogan!

Chris fell somewhere in the middle. God had given him a special talent but it lay in his feet rather than his patter. His natural reserve would come to the fore in a pub or social club. I recall his hand literally shaking as he held the mike to answer my first question but once he got into his stride, with the punters hanging on his every word, he was okay.

A glimpse into the future came when United played at Spurs towards the end of the year. It was the game which was to change his life.

In the second half Beardsley chipped the ball over and in one devastating move Waddle brought it down in the box, body swerved Paul Miller, and struck a shot firmly into the net past an admiring Ray Clemence. At that moment

Tottenham boss Peter Shreeves decided he must sign the big Geordie.

Afterwards he enthused: 'Some of the things he did were world class. He always frightened me when he had the ball.' Bobby Robson, once again in the stand, added: 'He makes some tremendous runs and gets behind people — and he scored a hell of a goal. He has a great touch.'

United had lost 3-1 but, more importantly, they had lost their biggest star whose contract was being allowed to expire. What followed didn't help things — Big Jack became obsessed with big centre-forwards and bought Tony Cunningham and George Reilly in quick succession.

Rumour had it that Charlton hadn't seen Cunningham play — he'd signed him on the recommendation of chief scout Maurice Setters — and that when he met him at the Central Station he didn't even know he was black! In any case, Jack quickly christened him Blackie Milburn much to the amusement of the players.

While two plodders were used in harness through the middle, the highly gifted Beardsley and Waddle were banished out to the wings to get round the back of defences and bang in crosses. Frankly, it was a waste of precious talent and did nothing to endear the manager to either of his future England internationals.

In fairness to Jack, who could be great company, he was a good organiser of teams and he kept United out of relegation trouble. But his style was to play it long and direct, eliminating players who liked to dwell on the ball, and it wasn't pretty to watch for the fans.

Waddle was to end up with 16 goals, one less than Beardsley, with the rest nowhere, but 15 of those 16 strikes had come before either Cunningham or Reilly had arrived. He felt that one of the big strikers should have been played with himself and Peter playing off him but the manager didn't want to know.

In the gathering gloom there was still some light, however. Waddle got his first full England call-up against Northern Ireland in February, 1985 though he was confined to the subs' bench but a month later made his debut in the 2-1 victory over Eire at Wembley. John Barnes was out through injury, thus enabling Chris to become the first Newcastle player since Malcolm Macdonald a decade before to turn out in the white of England and the first Geordie from United to be so honoured since the '50s.

While England beckoned, Waddle and Charlton were growing more apart. The big man ran United in a way few managers had before him — he was the gaffer and he took no interference from the boardroom. That was something the club had needed for a long time but, unfortunately, Charlton didn't use it to full advantage. He bought indifferently, using the club's cash as if it were his own and did exactly the same in contract negotiations with Chris.

Waddle never received the sort of offer which, after Charlton's disappearance, was made to both Beardsley and Gascoigne. Yet because he was the first of the trio out of the door he received more stick on his return to St. James's with Spurs than he ever deserved. I've always found it a source of wonderment that the likes of Beardsley and Paul Goddard could be welcomed back with such an open display of affection while Waddle was forced to run the gauntlet of the boo-boys.

His last season with United ended with official recognition of the part he had played. He was voted the *Evening Chronicle*-Hennessy Cognac North East Player of the Year and finished runner-up in the national PFA Young Player of the Year. Part of our prize was a weekend's trip to that most romantic of cities, Paris, and off we went with Hennessy representative Phillip Juniper and his wife Kay. I've made the trip four times with North East winners Jeff Clarke, Nick Pickering, Waddle and Beardsley and never tired of it once.

Hennessy are the most generous of hosts. We would fly from Newcastle on the Friday afternoon, linking up with Phillip and Kay at Heathrow, have a marvellous dinner at a restaurant on the Champs Elysées on the night, go shopping and sightseeing on the Saturday ending at the spectacular Lido Nightspot, and then do a final tour on the Sunday before flying back home.

With Chris and Lorna we indulged ourselves. We walked the Champs Elysées, climbed the Eiffel Tower, visited Montmartre with its quaint cafes and pavement artists, and took a boat down the Seine. On our particular night at the Lido we even met the Irish lady who formed the famed Bluebell Girls, 75-year-old Margaret Kelly, and Chris actually did a high-kicking routine with her for some publicity shots!

Phillip is football daft and a fervent Spurs supporter, so being with Waddle was a special joy for him. Though Chelsea were also in the frame for Chris it was obvious that he was going to White Hart Lane, though an independent tribunal actually fixed the fee much later at £590,000, which was a record for United.

At White Hart Lane the talent we had watched blossom reached full fruition. His debut saw him score twice against Watford in a 4-0 victory — surprisingly two headers — and he played in the 1987 F.A. Cup final against Coventry City but it was season 1988-89 which saw him alongside Gazza reach a consistency which placed him on a new plateau. Operating in a free role up front, Waddle conducted Terry Venables' orchestra with all the aplomb of a master craftsman.

His development off the park saw his horizons broaden beyond his wildest dreams. Why, he even appeared on *Top of the Pops* with his close mate Glenn Hoddle singing 'Diamond Lights', a record which reached No. 11 in the charts. A pop star was something the shy kid from the banks of the Tyne had never envisaged in his most extravagant moments.

England boss Bobby Robson never lost faith in him and, even though Barnes' development with Liverpool always played a restrictive role, Waddle represented his country in the 1986 World Cup finals in Mexico and 1988 European Championship finals in West Germany.

I've become a personal friend of Robson over the years and we've spent many an hour mulling over the merits of certain players. Bobby, a fellow Geordie, has never hesitated to label Waddle world-class yet never felt the same enthusiasm when discussing a fans' favourite like Hoddle.

That world-class tag was borne out in the summer of 1989 when Chris became the costliest player in the history of British football with a staggering £4.5m transfer to French champions Marseille. His contract guaranteed him £2m over four years — without any bonuses or endorsements which were certain to come his way. Not bad for a sausage seasoner from Gateshead!

WADDLE'S RECORD

190 appearances for United, scoring 52 goals. 169 in the League for 46 goals.
Second Division promotion in 1984 when he scored 18 goals in 42 outings.
F.A. Cup final appearance with Spurs 1987.
England appearances in the 1986 World Cup finals and 1988 European Championship finals.
North East Footballer of the Year 1985. Runner-up in the PFA Young Footballer of the Year.
United debut on October 22, 1980 v Shrewsbury. Won 1-0.

CHAPTER NINE

Peter Beardsley

One of my yearly tasks is to help out on presentation night at Wallsend Boys Club. It's nothing pretentious . . . a small room packed with mums, dads and kids with a bar at the back doing a big trade in orange juice and pints of lager for the fathers.

But there is one very significant difference. The old boys never fail to come home in their droves to honour the present crop of kids. Manchester United's Steve Bruce, Rob Hindmarch of Derby County, Everton's Neil McDonald, Eric Steele of Brighton and Derby fame, Les Sealey who was once at QPR, Ray Hankin (ex-Leeds), Mick Tait from Portsmouth . . . not one of 'em ever forgets his roots. And one Peter Beardsley, of Liverpool and England. A footballer who cost £1.8m in the transfer market.

Wallsend Boys Club, with a roll call of impressive quality and quantity, attracts scouts like bees round a honeypot. They're a ready source of raw talent. Yet Beardsley, the greatest to emerge from their ranks, couldn't find a club willing to take him. Gillingham gave him a trial and said no. So did Cambridge. And Burnley also turned him away.

Gerry Summers, then manager of Third Division Gillingham, told Beardsley bluntly: 'We don't think you have what it takes to make it as a pro.' And it was worse at Cambridge. He didn't last the week there before on the fourth day John Docherty declared: 'You might as well go home now. Our coach Peter Graham has to go up to Doncaster for a funeral and he'll drop you off at the station to get a train to Newcastle.' Despairing words for a youngster with a dream in his head but, my, how Messrs Summers and Docherty must have regretted them later!

Bob Moncur, who introduced Peter Beardsley to League soccer at Carlisle United, is pictured with his protégé at Gateshead Squash Club which Bob owned.

It was back to the factory floor at Killingworth and his £25-a-week job for Beardsley but the man who had shown faith in him, Wallsend Boys Club soccer leader Peter Kirkley, wouldn't accept defeat. It was Kirkley, later to be with Beardsley at St. James's as youth development officer, who had arranged the trips to Gillingham and Cambridge and he also got Peter down to Burnley, a club which had successfully raided the North East in the past.

The aspiring star, small and on the quiet side, trained with established players such as Leighton James, Martin Dobson, Frank Casper and Ray Hankin but failed to show the required qualities in an evening friendly.

It was now the summer of 1979 and the 18-year-old factory labourer was still nowhere near having his first foot on the ladder. Eventually Newcastle United came in with the offer of a trial, and after three days' training with them he was asked to play for Carlisle United in a friendly at Blue Star. Perhaps after so many failures it wasn't going to excite a youngster used to knockbacks but, in fact, it was to change his life. As I revealed in the chapter on Bob Moncur, the Carlisle manager liked what he saw and signed him on as a pro.

Slow beginnings, maybe, but once his foot was on the accelerator Beardsley wasted no time. A hat-trick for Carlisle reserves in his very first game against Wrexham catapulted him into a League debut on August 21, 1979 when Blackburn Rovers provided the opposition. That first season, 1979-80, Peter played 41 League games and was sub for two others, scoring 10 goals, and next time round his tally jumped to 15 as the headlines began to write themselves.

While Beardsley was beginning to make an impression at Carlisle, I was involved in a promotion to find the North East's Most Promising Newcomer. It was the brainchild of Peter Talbot, the enterprising manager of the Odeon Cinema in Newcastle. He had a sponsor and the idea was to hold a big sportsmen's dinner in the restaurant beneath the cinema with a celebrity handing over the trophy on the night. A short list would be drawn up with each star invited on the night and the winner kept a secret until the big moment.

Neat enough . . . except that I was to be the only judge. That particular year the finalists were Rob Hindmarch, skipper of Sunderland at the age of 19, British amateur ice-skating champion Karen Wood, local golfer David Hawkins, and Beardsley. I sat at the table with them knowing who had won and squirmed as it became apparent Rob fancied his chances, being captain of a top club, and Karen thought she was in with a great shout, having been brought all the way from Wales.

But to me Beardsley stood out head and shoulders above the rest and I believe I've been proved right since. His 'promise' has been fulfilled more than any other. Ironically he received his prize from Jack Charlton, later to become his manager at Newcastle and a source of conflict.

Peter was well chuffed and I did a big spread saying how much he would love to play for his home town club,

Newcastle. Nothing sensational in that, you might think, but the next morning the phone rang in the *Chronicle* offices and an irate Bob Stokoe bellowed: 'You're bloody well tapping my player.'

Now Bob can go off the deep end with pike and he wellied into me something awful, accusing me of luring his bright young star to St. James's. Evidentally Peter got the same treatment for his quotes.

Really, Bob loved Newcastle United as much as me. He played for them in the 1955 F.A. Cup final, and even when manager of their arch rivals Sunderland he would sit on the team coach at Roker Park long after the players had got off, following an away trip if United were on *Match of the Day.* We've kept in touch over the years but Stokoe is the worst loser I've ever met. If you beat him through the door he'd complain. And he felt he was losing Beardsley thanks to me.

In fact when Peter left Carlisle it was Bob who flogged him out of the country and across the Atlantic to Vancouver Whitecaps in a deal which many, including his old boss Bob Moncur, thought was plain daft as far as the player was concerned. Out of sight out of mind — he'd be lost in the gimmicky world of American soccer never to emerge again.

Beardsley, who had only flown once before to Holland with Wallsend Boys Club, signed a three-year contract with the Whitecaps taking him 6,000 miles away with a stipulation that he would go back to Carlisle in his first American close season.

'I didn't go for the money, I went for the experience,' said Beardsley. 'And I'm glad I did. Manager Johnny Giles was everything I thought he would be, a great player who knew how to pass on his knowledge to an avid pupil.'

In his first season abroad the Whitecaps won 20 of their 30 matches in the North American Soccer League with Peter fitting in like a glove with the likes of former Sunderland goalkeeper Barry Siddall, Welshman Terry Yorath and former Burnley and England winger Dave Thomas.

Second time around Manchester United were over for a four-team tournament and Beardsley took them apart. He scored in just 13 seconds and later hit a stunner — 'one of the best of my career', he called it.

Manchester United were beaten 3-1 and manager Ron Atkinson never forgot the little Geordie with the talented feet. By the September of 1982 Peter found himself at Old Trafford in a £250,000 'money back' deal. Atkinson was to assess him over the next six months, and if he was in the first team it would cost them another £50,000. If they sent him back to Canada they would get their money back.

It didn't quite turn out as Peter hoped. He was confined to only one first-team outing, against Third Division Bournemouth in the Milk Cup, and though Manchester United won 2-0, Beardsley was substituted 10 minutes from time. The trouble was Atkinson already had two bright young strikers in Norman Whiteside, then only 17 but already a World Cup star with Northern Ireland, and Mark Hughes, who cost £2m when Barcelona signed him. So it was back to Vancouver for a final season and a second successive Player of the Year award.

By now Arthur Cox was building a Second Division promotion side round Kevin Keegan at Newcastle. He needed another piece of the jigsaw — someone to play up front with KK. Imre Varadi had been sold, and he'd failed to get George Reilly. His thoughts turned across the Atlantic to Beardsley.

A £120,000 deal was set up with the Whitecaps and, having been alerted to the situation, I phoned up my Most Promising Newcomer in Vancouver. Would he like to come to Newcastle? Would he!

On the night of September 20, 1983 Beardsley touched down at Newcastle Airport on the last leg of his flight to Canada. He was home at last and promotion for United was less than eight months away.

Beardsley was to revere Keegan in the way a son looks up to a father. It was Kevin who christened him Pedro — a name which stuck — and it was Kevin who taught him how to handle stardom.

No one can get near Beardsley as he dances between three Barnsley defenders including former Nottingham Forest and Scotland star Kenny Burns on the right.

'He wasn't simply kind and helpful, he was an inspirational figure who really marked my card about the kind of future I might have if I followed his example,' said Beardsley. 'Kevin had charisma. He was magic to play with, terrific to train with and away from the game he conducted himself with humour, grace and dignity.'

Like Peter, the great man had a sweet tooth and when United played at Manchester City in a key promotion game a fan handed Keegan a box of toffees on the way in.

'They didn't last long,' recalls Beardsley. 'As we got changed he ate toffee after toffee. They had all gone before he led us out — hardly the ideal preparation for a big match, you might think. But as usual he came up with the goods, scoring one of our goals in a great 2-1 victory before almost 42,000 spectators.'

The only game Keegan missed in United's promotion season was, ironically, the one which mathematically clinched things at Huddersfield. On the way down Cox asked Beardsley: 'How would you like to wear Kevin's No. 7 shirt?' To Peter it was the highest accolade possible and he went out to score in the 2-2 draw which took Newcastle up.

But with Keegan's retirement and Cox's departure came a transformation for Peter. First Division soccer was tempered by the arrival of Jack Charlton, a manager who failed to win the heart of one of his best players.

In a book entitled *Proud to be a Geordie* Beardsley wrote: 'It didn't take me long to become disenchanted. It quickly became evident that Jack liked the ball kicked long from the back, a ploy which did little for the morale of our midfield operators and hardly endeared him to the front runners. But the lowest ebb of my relationship — if you can call it a relationship — with big Jack came about with two incidents in successive home games in late February and early March.

'We were beating Luton Town by the only goal at home and with just a few seconds left I received the ball. Immediately I began to make tracks towards their defence and when the whistle went for the end of the game I was just happy that we'd picked up three valuable points. But my elation was rudely shattered when Jack Charlton strode onto the pitch grabbed me by the arm and gave me a right going over for messing about. It was the most embarrassing moment I've had in the game.

'Glenn Roeder stepped between us and told the manager to save his comments for the dressing-room. I do recognise the manager's rights to make his point to any player and I've certainly never considered myself above criticism. But I will always believe that Jack was wrong to set about me on the pitch.

'A week later he did have the grace to wait until I went down the tunnel before giving me another rollocking. This time we were leading Watford 2-1 with just a few seconds left. When we were awarded a free-kick I took it quickly, chipped the ball into the danger area and George Reilly headed our third.

'I was really pleased with myself — George was also chuffed to score against his old mates — but again that emotion lasted only a few seconds. I had left the pitch — but only just — when Jack steamed in again. Apparently he believed that I should have kicked the ball out towards the corner flag from the free-kick. I felt I just couldn't win — and I wasn't too fussed about winning if we had to resort to such negative tactics.

'Those two incidents sharpened my awareness that Jack and I would never be on the same wavelength.'

Beardsley has more than a point but in fairness it must be emphasised that Charlton has made a habit throughout his managerial career of getting results with a particular style of play. He did it at Middlesbrough, Sheffield Wednesday, Newcastle and with the Eire inter-national side. He'd been brought up at Leeds where Don Revie had professionalism down to an art form — you didn't tell the opposition the time of day — and that, coupled with a fiery temper, led to many clashes. Big Jack did it his way and he was no respecter of players, even if they were stars.

Whenever we've done talk-ins together he's started off by saying to supporters: 'I won't argue. I'll tell you what I think and that's it.' Many's the time a highly indignant fan has begun his question: 'I know you don't care what we think but . . .'

When Big Jack quit after being barracked in a pre-season friendly Beardsley ploughed in: 'I'm no hypocrite and I shed no crocodile tears. I think Jack bottled it — he thought he was above criticism.'

Waddle left during Charlton's short reign and Beardsley admits that if his contract had expired then (it still had a year to run) he would certainly have gone too. The elevation of Willie McFaul to manager prevented that and the following season Peter signed a new two-year deal.

McFaul represented an easing of pressure and Beardsley, progressing anyway despite the trials and tribulations, blossomed into a full England international in

Willie's first season. It was to lead him to the Mexico World Cup finals of 1986 even though he was a latecomer to the national set-up. Once he gets going the little fella with the jutting jaw makes rapid strides.

His England debut was against Egypt in Cairo at the start of the year, the sort of gentle introduction Bobby Robson likes to give his newcomers. He went on as sub for Gary Lineker 10 minutes into the second half and a month later played the full 90 minutes in Israel alongside Kerry Dixon. The result: 2-1.

March brought the major breakthrough. Russia were the opposition in Tblisi and, because of injuries, Beardsley lined up as partner to Lineker in what was to become a brilliant twosome. That match, beamed back home on telly, was won for England by a 'Newcastle' goal — Beardsley chased a ball wide on the right towards the corner flag, won it off the Russian defender with the sort of sliding drag-back tackle once the trademark of Jackie Milburn and, looking up, crossed perfectly into the path of Chris Waddle for a picture goal.

From then on Beardsley was a regular in the England squad and at the beginning of May was on the plane out of Gatwick bound for Colorado Springs and high-altitude training before the World Cup finals in Mexico. United had finished 11th in the League with Peter an ever-present, scoring 19 First Division goals.

Bobby Robson called him 'my little gem' and so he was. After a stuttering start against Portugal and Morocco Beardsley was brought off the subs' bench and into the team and England powered through to the quarter-finals before the Hand of God, in the shape of Argentina's Maradona, intervened.

It was a packed summer of high drama for Peter but we still managed to shoehorn into it a weekend in Paris to celebrate him being voted the North East Player of the Year. It was basically the same routine I'd gone through with Waddle 12 months before but it was nonetheless enjoyable. And even in the packed roadside cafes of

Beardsley beats Paraguay keeper Roberto Fernandez to score England's second goal during the 1986 World Cup finals in Mexico.

Montmartre Peter was recognised and asked for his autograph.

But there was to be only one more season of Beardsley at Newcastle before he followed Waddle out of the door marked exit.

The parting was long drawn-out and somewhat painful. It was natural after the Waddle affair that United's fans would be worried and their fears were well founded. Peter was offered the sort of contract Waddle never saw but he steadfastly refused to sign it and in the summer of 1987 he joined Liverpool for a staggering £1.8m.

There is no question that things were strained long before the transfer, which was one of the worst-kept secrets in football. McFaul felt somewhat let down and so did the United players including his close friend Glenn Roeder. Albert Craig, a mediocre midfield player who had come down from Scotland, made matters worse by stating publicly that Beardsley's team-mates were jealous of his success.

Peter never said a word but Olympic medallist Brendan Foster, a great Newcastle supporter, told me afterwards of flying to London with Beardsley who, once he knew Bren was on his way out of the country to America, admitted he was going to join Liverpool.

A lot was said, and has been said since, about loyalty but the harsh facts of life have to be faced. A top player can command top wages anywhere but what United couldn't guarantee Beardsley was success. Sadly for us Liverpool could, and within one season Peter had won the First Division championship and appeared in the F.A. Cup final. He might not have achieved that in a full career at Newcastle. It was sad for me and for everyone who loved United that such a fine player left, but in what is a short career a player must look after himself. Until United match the ambition of their fans they will continue to lose men of quality.

George Best, one of the greatest ever British players, summed up the talent of Beardsley when he said: 'I liked him from the moment I first saw him. He was a bit of an unknown then playing for one of the American teams but he made an electrifying impression on me. He simply oozed class and skill and his first touch to bring a ball under control instantly was a real eye-opener. I've seen a lot of him since then and he has never failed to impress me.

'Negative players are ruining the game. As soon as they get the ball they want to give it to someone else because they don't know what to do with it. You could never accuse Beardsley of that. He actually wants to get himself into trouble, if you know what I mean, by his willingness to take on defenders.

'He's backing his ability to come out a winner — and that helps him do the business for Liverpool and England. Even when he hasn't got the ball he's still always available. He

Peter and Sandra Beardsley, along with author John Gibson, enjoy an ice cream in front of the Eiffel Tower during the trip to Paris as part of Beardsley's prize for being voted North East Player of the Year.

takes all the stick in the world and still comes back for more — and the result is defenders can never relax.

'Even when he's having a quiet game by his own standards he's likely to create something of pure genius, beating two or three guys and then sticking it in the net. You need skill and brains to create space in the danger areas. Most players lack one or the other but Beardsley has plenty of both.'

Enough said.

PETER BEARDSLEY'S RECORD

102 League appearances for Carlisle, scoring 22 goals, and 147 League outings for United, notching 61 goals.
North East Player of the Year 1986.
First Division championship with Liverpool 1988.

F.A. Cup final with Liverpool 1988.
England player in 1986 World Cup finals in Mexico and 1988 European Championship finals in West Germany.
Record transfer fee of £1.8m from United to Liverpool in 1987.

CHAPTER TEN

Paul Gascoigne

Geoff Wilson, who ran the under 15 team at Heathfield High School in Gateshead, remembers the young Gascoigne.

'He had a round face, round body and round legs. But I've never seen so much skill in a young player — it was amazing.'

Amazing, maybe, but the kid with the broad grin and the broad beam didn't find the path into the Football League terribly easy. Born at Teams, a tough but friendly area on the banks of the Tyne, he played for Dunston Juniors under the guidance of another early influence, Alf Pringle, and represented both Gateshead and Durham Boys without having League clubs exactly falling over themselves to sign him on. Indeed Ipswich Town, then managed by Bobby Robson who was later to cap him for England, Middlesbrough and Southampton all rejected him before Newcastle United took the plunge.

Willie McFaul had seen him play for his school but it was youth development officer Peter Kirkley, who had shown such faith in Peter Beardsley, who was convinced the lad had a future in the professional game.

'He was small and chubby and a bit of a plodder,' recalls Kirkley. 'But he had exceptional skill. There was something about him that made you feel good.'

Gazza has always been prone to carry a few extra pounds but in his early days with United he was a positive porker. In fact his craving for junk food led to him almost being booted out of the club before he got started.

'I was hooked on sweet things,' admitted Paul. 'Mars bars, ice creams, cans of pop, mince pies, the lot. I used to stuff them all down. I would sit in front of the TV gorging myself silly. I thought it would be okay because I'd be able to burn off the extra calories. But I became podgy.'

Jack Charlton, then United's boss, had different ideas. He called Gazza into his office and told him bluntly: 'Get that excess weight off in a fortnight or you're out on your ear.' Gascoigne was scared of the big man with the gruff voice — so scared that he lost half a stone in a week and his career was saved.

He had been an apprentice in the Kevin Keegan glory days at St. James's and, like so many kids, revered the former England skipper.

He was assigned to look after Keegan's boots and one day Kevin gave him three pairs of boots to break in wearing round the house, but Gazza lost one of them on the way home.

'I was on the Metro showing Keegan's boots to some of my mates. But when I got home I discovered one was missing. I panicked. I went back to the Metro, looking round all the stations, and I searched the bus I'd also travelled on. But I couldn't find the boot anywhere. I thought I'd be sacked. I was in a blind panic and chickened out, asking my dad to tell Kevin what had happened. But Kevin was great — he just shrugged and said he hadn't liked the boots anyway.'

It was during Charlton's short one-season reign as Newcastle's manager that Gascoigne made his big impression, however. United won the F.A. Youth Cup for only the second time in their history, 23 years after Bob Moncur, David Craig and Alan Suddick first achieved such national recognition, and it was Gazza who was the inspirational skipper.

In the two-legged final Watford had achieved the hard bit, drawing 0-0 at St. James's Park but in the return, despite going one down, United stormed to a 4-1 victory with Gascoigne and striker Joe Allon scoring two goals apiece.

Paul looks back: 'I scored one of my best goals at

A young Paul Gascoigne (left) holds the F.A. Youth Cup with striker Joe Allon after they had both scored twice to help United beat Watford in the final.

Vicarage Road playing a couple of one-twos with Tony Hayton and Joe Allon to chip the keeper. It felt good.'

In the dressing-room afterwards Watford chairman Elton John interrupted the celebrations to offer his own congratulations. Most of the Newcastle youngsters were a little bit in awe of the pop superstar but not Gazza.

He broke the nervous silence when he piped up from the back: 'Give us a song, Elton!' The cheeky chappie was on his way.

Gascoigne had made a couple of First Division appearances under Big Jack as a sub but his full League debut came in Willie McFaul's first match as manager at Southampton at the beginning of season 1985-86. Pat Heard was dropped, in went Gazza, and United snatched a draw.

It was a season when Beardsley was the No. 1 star with another fledgling, winger Paul Stephenson, flickering brightly along with the precocious Gascoigne, who underlined his budding talent by scoring nine times in 28 appearances. United finished comfortably in a mid-table 11th place though McFaul found it that much more difficult in his second season until two men rescued him from the jaws of relegation — £415,000 striker Paul Goddard and Gascoigne.

By the end of the February United were anchored at the foot of the First Division, having taken only one point from their last nine matches. They appeared to have as much chance of staying up as a snowflake of surviving in the Sahara. But then the G force blew away the clouds of despair. Gascoigne, still tender of years but with talent to spare, emerged from nearly five months out with a bad groin strain to bring an inventive flair into midfield and Goddard, a fine team player and target man, went off on a goal rampage. He scored in seven successive outings — all key goals in tight matches — to guarantee survival but the unbearable pressure told on both the players and the crowd.

In one match the normally placid Goddard actually grabbed Gazza by the throat after he had created an opening out of nothing, jinking his way through a wrong-footed defence, but then, having beaten the keeper, he tried to turn it into a wonder goal, allowing the keeper to get back and retrieve the situation.

It was the inexperience of youth coupled with the showmanship of an artist combining to produce his downfall. Gazza, emerging as a clown prince of soccer, couldn't resist the final flourish when an act of simplicity was all that was required. It could have cost United crucial points but, on the other hand, it's the player with the ability and courage to try something different who entertains and often wins matches through his special gift.

On occasions Gascoigne was to infuriate his fellow team-mates and his manager, but with Beardsley on his way to Liverpool at the end of that season he was to take over the mantle of top dog at St. James's.

That, despite being only 20 and despite the fact that United in August 1987 paid more than half a million pounds to bring Brazil's international centre-forward Mirandinha from South America. Mira was the first Brazilian to play in the Football League in its 100-year history and his totally unexpected arrival was to excite not only Tyneside but the whole of the country. He went off like a bomb, his blistering speed terrorising defenders as he rattled up 11 goals by Christmas but Mira was to fade alarmingly and it was Gascoigne who produced the Brazilian style first-touch soccer of swaying passes, devastating body swerves and banana free-kicks.

Mira and Gazza — two individuals with a high belief in themselves — were to argue like crazy on the field. Each believed the other wouldn't pass him the salt never mind the ball. It was seen by the crowd, it made the papers, and it created quite a talking point.

I know them both well and as a matter of fact I had them both on stage together at talk-ins more than once at the height of the alleged controversy. Off the park they would laugh at the furore, accusing each other jokingly, one in broad Geordie and the other in broken English. I doubt if anyone in the audience could understand a word!

Mira called Gazza 'the crazy one', and when Paul said his goldfish looked just like the little Brazilian with his mouth open Mira replied: 'I've just bought a dog. It's crazy, too. That's why I call it Gazza!'

One night when they were together at Ponteland Social Club Paul ended our session by sitting down at the organ on stage and treating us all to a medley of rock and roll hits. The punters couldn't believe it — they loved the kid with a down-to-earth attitude saying, 'Let's have a sing song to round off the night.'

Paul was totally unpredictable, sometimes infuriating, but always fun. I once arranged to pick him up at Jesmond Tennis Club to do a chat show at Ashington. I emphasised the time and the importance of not keeping the audience waiting and Gazza said aye, not to worry. When I walked through the gate there was Paul still on court playing a mixed doubles match. He winked, won a couple of points to tie up the match, and then ran across with sweat pouring off him. He'd left his suit back home in Dunston and we'd have to nip back for him to get changed.

He drove like someone demented, waving cheerily at everyone on every street corner, until we made his house. Upstairs he ran about, shouting to his mam for his newly ironed shirt only to discover that his dad had put it on and gone off to the social club! Eventually he emerged to inform me that we'd have to go round to his girlfriend's — he'd left the jacket of his suit there the night before. By now I was bordering on hysteria but Gazza was as happy-go-lucky as a punter with the pools up. The drive to Ashington seemed like an eternity and we were met outside the club by a bunch of officials looking in desperation for a sign of their lost performers.

We went on stage in front of a fidgety audience well over an hour late but Paul soon charmed them with a succession of daft tales about how he booked a sun bed course for black centre-forward Tony Cunningham. It's hard to be angry when you're laughing!

Gazza was exactly the same on the field. At Arsenal he gave England midfielder Steve Williams the run-around for 90 minutes to set up a famous Newcastle victory, and as they trudged off at the end he tugged at an imaginary pocket in his shorts declaring: 'It's all right, you can come out now, Stevie.'

Then when Manchester United stuck the tenacious Remi Moses on him at the park Paul looked down at him after another tackle had failed and said: 'Remi, you're like dog's muck — you're always under everybody's feet.'

And when he clashed with 41-year-old Billy Bonds of West Ham he asked: 'All right, Billy?' Bonds replied: 'It's my ankle', to which came the retort: 'Oh, good. I thought it might be arthritis.'

A typical Gazza pose after scoring a goal for United.

Chris Waddle, now a team mate at Spurs, insists: 'Some people might think he's taking the Michael but there's no malice in Gazza.' However, I know that Glenn Roeder, who protected him and advised him like a father, was always worried that some thug who had been given the run-around by a cocky kid would take his own retribution in the next match and break his leg. The thought never seemed to cross Paul's mind.

While he seemed brash and even a loudmouth, I knew another side to Gazza. Not only would he give you his last penny but he was as soft as putty underneath. He could easily be hurt.

At yet another talk-in at the height of his fame with United we were at Morpeth along with Paul Goddard. Gascoigne wowed the packed audience with his one-liners and a succession of jokes that had nowt to do with football but would have made local comedians like Spike Rawlings or Bobby Pattinson proud. Then, right at the death, a punter asked a question about the money supposedly offered to Paul to stay at Newcastle.

'I'm an out of work miner but I spend my dole money to watch you on a Saturday,' he said with feeling. 'Yet you turn down £2,000 a week to stay at the town.'

Gazza answered quickly. I wrapped the show up, and we were off stage. At the reception in the back room Paul went missing and with a queue of fans waiting for his autograph I went looking for him. He was locked in a toilet cubicle with tears rolling down his cheeks. The thought of a working-class lad like himself thinking he was too big for his boots destroyed him. I had to wipe away the tears with a piece of toilet paper and help him pull himself together before he could come out to face his admirers.

It was at the same show, incidentally, that Gazza inadvertently got the Newcastle United talk-ins banned. In response to another question from the floor on his future he had got stuck into what he called the lack of ambition in the boardroom and said that could be the one factor to drive him out. His honesty brought a round of applause but, unknown to us all, a neighbour of the then chairman Stan Seymour who lived in Morpeth was in the audience and the word got back to headquarters. The next thing I heard was that the players had been stopped from appearing, which was a great shame because, in the main, they were fine ambassadors for the club, bridging the gap between the dressing-room and the supporters. They weren't inaccessible stars but on the same level as those who paid to watch them.

In his last season as a Magpie United finished a creditable eighth with a late flurry of results but, as with Waddle and Beardsley before him, the talk on the terraces was all of their top player leaving even though he had another year of his contract to go.

Gazza's impishness, his showmanship, was rewarded when he was voted our North East Player of the Year and nationally lifted the PFA's Young Player of the Year. He was an established member of England's Under 21 international team and it all led to a thirst for medals which could be won on faraway battlefields.

There was no question that Gascoigne wanted to tread the path of Beardsley to Liverpool but the champions, well stocked in midfield, weren't in a rush to take a 21-year-old however talented. That left Spurs and Manchester United in a two-way battle. Roeder felt that his prodigy would be best served by staying another two years at United and feared for him in the bright lights of London. But the dye had been cast, Paul had made his stand, and it was Tottenham who met the asking price, a staggering record £2m for a player yet to win a full England cap.

Potential had never come so dear and Gascoigne, perhaps not surprisingly, was greeted with a welter of bad publicity when he arrived on the doorstep of Fleet Street in the close season of 1988. Here was an arrogant but highly likeable young kid used to being able to go for a pint at his local or Tuxedo nightclub without causing a flicker suddenly thrust into the centre of attention. Standing with a pint in his hand laughing loudly with his Geordie mates, he was so liable to create the wrong impression in tabloids looking for a sensational story. All the fears of Roeder seemed to be coming true.

By sheer coincidence Spurs' first match against Coventry was postponed because their new stand wasn't safe — and that meant his debut was at Newcastle. He was greeted with a barrage of Mars bars thrown onto the pitch, taunted with chants of 'Fat boy' and substituted with cramp before the end.

But slowly his ability began to come through and the stories changed from off-the-field eye-openers to on-field joy. Gascoigne was hailed for his entertainment value in a time of anonymous, grey players. He blew kisses to opponents, stuck his tongue out at referees and shoved the ball up his jersey to conduct the terrace chants of 'Fat boy'.

Waddle enthused: 'Gazza has always been the same and always will be. He loves entertaining the crowd but it's not an act. He's exactly the same personality in training when he doesn't have an audience. And I can't see it ever being knocked out of him. He really is a one-off in this day and age.'

Glenn Hoddle, who had found it hard under ex-United coach Keith Burkinshaw to keep his own individuality, saw Gascoigne as the new hope that the system can, in fact, be bucked.

'The best thing that could happen is for Spurs to win a major trophy with Gazza the star of the show. Perhaps then it would convince other managers and coaches to play the game based on skill and entertainment.'

Gascoigne himself saw his role in simple terms. 'If I achieve anything in my career it would be nice to put a smile back on the face of soccer. People want to be entertained and excited and if they think I'm a showman that's okay by me. If I thought someone looked at a newspaper, saw I was playing in town and came along to watch, that would give me a lot of satisfaction. There isn't a man in this country who doesn't like a laugh and I think football should be fun.'

Gazza proudly wears his England Under 21 international cap.

Bobby Robson introduced Gazza to the full England team via substitute appearances during his first season at Spurs and we talked at length about the Geordie boy with the touch of genius when I visited the Football Association headquarters at Lancaster Gate in London.

'He's the most precocious youngster I've ever met in my life,' Bobby told me. 'He could be exceptional as a player. Gazza is a real Jack the Lad but we mustn't take too much of that away from him. All the great players — George Best, Bobby Charlton and Denis Law — had that burning self-belief and so has Gascoigne.'

He recalled with relish a couple of stories about the newcomer in England's squad. Prior to a big international at Wembley Robson took the England players to a snooty golf club in Surrey to play a round and then have dinner. Bobby made a formal speech which was responded to by the club captain. All very sedate and nice.

It's no good looking — an opponent is left for dead by Gascoigne's skills.

'Then for some reason someone suggested that Gazza should have a few words. He was the youngest member of the international squad, but far from being overawed he got up and told a succession of dirty stories that completely broke the ice and had the whole place in uproar.'

Then in a friendly international in Saudi Arabia, with Robson's job under fire, the England boss decided to throw him on with quarter of an hour to go and the game delicately poised at 1-1.

'I told him I didn't want to lose the game and that he must work back defensively. But I also told him I wanted to win if possible.

'He simply looked at me and said 'I'll get you a goal,

gaffer.' And he meant it. He may be only a kid but he knows what he's capable of.'

Trevor Brooking, like so many, is an admirer of Gascoigne. 'The final product could turn out to be breath-taking,' said Trevor, but he summed up the feeling of us all when he added: 'It all depends if he can keep his feet on the ground.'

PAUL GASCOIGNE'S RECORD

92 League games for United, scoring 21 goals.
F.A. Youth Cup winner 1985 as captain, scoring two goals in the final against Watford.
North East Player of the Year 1988.
PFA Young Player of the Year 1988.
Full England international with Spurs 1988-89.
Record transfer fee of £2m from United to Spurs in 1988.
Debut v Southampton 1985.

Club Honours

Football League champions: 1905, 1907, 1909, 1927.
Football League Division Two champions: 1965.
F.A. Cup winners: 1910, 1924, 1932, 1951, 1952, 1955.
F.A. Cup finalists: 1905, 1906, 1908, 1911, 1974.
League Cup finalists: 1976.
European Fairs Cup winners: 1969.
Texaco Cup winners: 1974, 1975.
Anglo Italian Cup winners: 1973.
F.A. Charity Shield winners: 1909.
Record League victory: 13-0 v Newport County, Division Two, October 5, 1946.
Record Cup victory: 9-0 v Southport, F.A. Cup fourth round replay, 1932.
Record League defeat: 0-9 v Burton Wanderers, Division Two, April 15, 1895.
Record Cup defeat: 1-7 v Aston Villa, F.A. Cup second round, 1895.
Most League goals: 98, season 1951-2, Division One, position 8th.
Record attendance: 68,586 v Chelsea, Division One, September 3, 1930.
Record goalscorer in one League season: Hughie Gallacher, 36, 1926-27.
Most goals in a match: Len Shackleton, six, v Newport County, October 5, 1946.
Most appearances: Jimmy Lawrence, 495, 1904-22.
Best aggregate number of goals: Jackie Milburn 221 (199 League and 22 F.A. Cup).

F.A. Cup Winning Teams

1910 (2-0 v Barnsley after 1-1 draw): Lawrence, McCracken, Whitson; Veitch, Low W., McWilliam; Rutherford, Howie, Shepherd, Higgins, Wilson.
In the replay as above except Carr for Whitson. Goalscorer: Shepherd 2.

1924 (2-0 v Aston Villa): Bradley; Hampson, Hudspeth; Gibson, Spencer, Mooney; Low J., Cowen, Harris N., McDonald, Seymour. Goalscorers: Harris, Seymour.
1932 (2-1 v Arsenal): McInroy; Nelson, Fairhurst; McKenzie, Davidson, Weaver; Boyd, Richardson, Allen, McMenemy, Lang. Goalscorer: Allen 2.
1951 (2-0 v Blackpool): Fairbrother; Cowell, Corbett; Harvey, Brennan, Crowe; Walker, Taylor, Milburn, Robledo G., Mitchell. Goalscorer: Milburn 2.
1952 (1-0 v Arsenal): Simpson; Cowell, McMichael; Harvey, Brennan, Robledo E.; Walker, Foulkes, Milburn, Robledo G., Mitchell. Goalscorer: Robledo G.
1955 (3-1 v Manchester City): Simpson; Cowell, Batty; Scoular, Stokoe, Casey; White, Milburn, Keeble, Hannah, Mitchell. Goalscorers: Milburn, Hannah, Mitchell.

European Fairs Cup Winning Team
1969 (v Ujpest Dozsa 3-0 and 3-2, 6-2 on agg): McFaul; Craig, Clark; Gibb, Burton, Moncur; Scott, Robson, Davies, Arentoft, Sinclair. Sub: Foggon. Goalscorers: Moncur 2 and Scott in first leg at St. James's Park; Moncur, Arentoft and Foggon in second leg in Hungary.

Football League Record

Division II	*P*	*W*	*D*	*L*	*F*		*A*	*Pts*	*Posn*	*Top Scorer*	
1893-94	28	15	6	7	66	-	39	36	4th	THOMPSON W	19
1894-95	30	12	3	15	72	-	84	27	10th	THOMPSON W	17
1895-96	30	16	2	12	73	-	50	34	5th	WARDROPE W	22
1896-97	30	17	1	12	56	-	52	35	5th	SMELLIE R	17
1897-98	30	21	3	6	64	-	32	45	2nd	PEDDIE J	18

Division I	*P*	*W*	*D*	*L*	*F*		*A*	*Pts*	*Posn*	*Top Scorer*	
1898-99	34	11	8	15	48	-	48	30	13th	PEDDIE J	19
1899-1900	34	13	10	11	53	-	43	36	5th	PEDDIE J	16
1900-01	34	14	10	10	42	-	37	38	6th	PEDDIE J	14
1901-02	34	14	9	11	48	-	34	37	3rd	ROBERTS R	12
1902-03	34	14	4	16	41	-	51	32	14th	McCOLL R S	10
1903-04	34	18	6	10	58	-	45	42	4th	APPLEYARD W	15
1904-05	34	23	2	9	72	-	33	48	1st	APPLEYARD W	13
1905-06	38	18	7	13	74	-	48	43	4th	ORR R	17

Division I	*P*	*W*	*D*	*L*	*F*	*A*	*Pts*	*Posn*	*Top Scorer*	Goals
1906-07	38	22	7	9	74	46	51	1st	APPLEYARD W	17
1907-08	38	15	12	11	65	54	42	4th	APPLEYARD W	14
1908-09	38	24	5	9	65	41	53	1st	SHEPHERD A	12
1909-10	38	19	7	12	70	56	45	4th	SHEPHERD A	29
1910-11	38	15	10	13	61	43	40	8th	SHEPHERD A	25
1911-12	38	18	8	12	64	50	44	3rd	STEWART - HIBBERT	11
1912-13	38	13	8	17	47	47	34	14th	STEWART J	9
1913-14	38	13	11	14	39	48	37	11th	SHEPHERD A	10
1914-15	38	11	10	17	46	48	32	15th	HIBBERT W	16
1919-20	42	17	9	16	44	39	43	8th	SMAILES A	10
1920-21	42	20	10	12	66	45	50	5th	SMAILES A	18
1921-22	42	18	10	14	59	45	46	7th	HARRIS N	22
1922-23	42	18	12	12	45	37	48	4th	McDONALD T	15
1923-24	42	17	10	15	60	54	44	9th	SEYMOUR S	16
1924-25	42	16	16	10	61	42	48	6th	HARRIS N	20
1925-26	42	16	10	16	84	75	42	10th	GALLACHER H	23
1926-27	42	25	6	11	96	58	56	1st	GALLACHER H	36
1927-28	42	15	13	14	79	81	43	9th	GALLACHER H	21
1928-29	42	19	6	17	70	72	44	10th	GALLACHER H	23
1929-30	42	15	7	20	71	92	37	19th	GALLACHER H	29
1930-31	42	15	6	21	78	87	36	17th	LINDSAY - BEDFORD	12
1931-32	42	18	6	18	80	87	42	11th	BOYD J	18
1932-33	42	22	5	15	71	63	49	5th	ALLAN J	19
1933-34	42	10	14	18	68	77	34	21st	WEAVER S	14
Division II	*P*	*W*	*D*	*L*	*F*	*A*	*Pts*	*Posn*	*Top Scorer*	
1934-35	42	22	4	16	89	68	48	6th	SMITH J	16
1935-36	42	20	6	16	88	79	46	8th	SMITH J	22
1936-37	42	22	5	15	80	56	49	4th	SMITH J	25
1937-38	42	14	8	20	51	58	36	19th	IMRIE-PARK	9
1938-39	42	18	10	14	61	48	46	9th	CAIRNS W	19
1946-47	42	19	10	13	95	62	48	5th	WAYMAN C	30
1947-48	42	24	8	10	72	41	56	2nd	MILBURN J	21
Division I	*P*	*W*	*D*	*L*	*F*	*A*	*Pts*	*Posn*	*Top Scorer*	
1948-49	42	20	12	10	70	56	52	4th	MILBURN J	19
1949-50	42	19	12	11	77	55	50	5th	MILBURN J	18
1950-51	42	18	13	11	62	53	49	4th	MILBURN J	17
1951-52	42	18	9	15	98	73	45	8th	ROBLEDO G	33

Division I	*P*	*W*	*D*	*L*	*F*		*A*	*Pts*	*Posn*	*Top Scorer*	
1952-53	42	14	9	19	59	-	70	37	16th	ROBLEDO G	18
1953-54	42	14	10	18	72	-	77	38	15th	MILBURN J	16
1954-55	42	17	9	16	89	-	77	43	8th	MILBURN - MITCHELL	19
1955-56	42	17	7	18	85	-	70	41	11th	KEEBLE V	26
1956-57	42	14	8	20	67	-	87	36	17th	DAVIES R	13
1957-58	42	12	8	22	73	-	81	32	19th	WHITE L	22
1958-59	42	17	7	18	80	-	80	41	11th	WHITE L	25
1959-60	42	18	8	16	82	-	78	44	8th	WHITE L	28
1960-61	42	11	10	21	86	-	109	32	21st	WHITE L	28

Division II	*P*	*W*	*D*	*L*	*F*		*A*	*Pts*	*Posn*	*Top Scorer*	
1961-62	42	15	9	18	64	-	58	39	11th	ALLCHURCH - THOMAS	10
1962-63	42	18	11	13	79	-	59	47	7th	THOMAS-FELL	15
1963-64	42	20	5	17	74	-	69	45	8th	THOMAS B	20
1964-65	42	24	9	9	81	-	45	57	1st	McGARRY R	16

Division I	*P*	*W*	*D*	*L*	*F*		*A*	*Pts*	*Posn*	*Top Scorer*	
1965-66	42	14	9	19	50	-	63	37	15th	SUDDICK A	14
1966-67	42	12	9	21	39	-	81	33	20th	ROBSON B	10
1967-68	42	13	15	14	54	-	67	41	10th	DAVIES W	12
1968-69	42	15	14	13	61	-	55	44	9th	ROBSON B	21
1969-70	42	17	13	12	57	-	35	47	7th	ROBSON B	22
1970-71	42	14	13	15	44	-	46	41	12th	ROBSON B	9
1971-72	42	15	11	16	49	-	45	41	11th	MACDONALD M	23
1972-73	42	16	13	13	60	-	51	45	8th	TUDOR J	18
1973-74	42	13	12	17	49	-	48	38	15th	MACDONALD M	15
1974-75	42	15	9	18	59	-	72	39	15th	MACDONALDM	21
1975-76	42	15	9	18	71	-	62	39	15th	MACDONALD M	19
1976-77	42	18	13	11	64	-	49	49	5th	BURNS M	14
1977-78	42	6	10	26	42	-	78	22	21st	BURNS M	15

Division II	*P*	*W*	*D*	*L*	*F*		*A*	*Pts*	*Posn*	*Top Scorer*	
1978-79	42	17	8	17	51	-	55	42	8th	WITHE P	14
1979-80	42	15	14	13	53	-	49	44	9th	SHOULDER A	20
1980-81	42	14	14	14	33	-	45	42	11th	SHINTON R	7
1981-82	42	18	8	16	52	-	50	62	9th	VARADI I	18
1982-83	42	18	13	11	75	-	53	67	5th	VARADI I	21
1983-84	42	24	8	10	85	-	53	80	3rd	KEEGAN K	27

Division I	*P*	*W*	*D*	*L*	*F*		*A*	*Pts*	*Posn*	*Top Scorer*	
1984-85	42	13	13	16	55	-	70	52	14th	BEARDSLEY P	17
1985-86	42	17	12	13	67	-	72	63	11th	BEARDSLEY P	19
1986-87	42	12	11	19	47	-	65	47	17th	GODDARD P	11
1987-88	40	14	14	12	55	-	53	56	8th	O'NEILL M	12
1988-89	38	7	10	21	32	-	63	31	20th	MIRANDINHA	11